Michael Faulkner grew up in Northern Ireland but has spent most of his adult life in Scotland, initially working as a solicitor and subsequently setting up the UK's first company to design, manufacture and retail Santa Fe-style furniture.

In 2002 Mike and his wife Lynn McGregor, a professional artist, moved to the cabin on Islandmore, Strangford Lough, his family's summer home.

Mike's acclaimed first book, *The Blue Cabin: Living by the Tides on Islandmore*, was published by Blackstaff Press in 2006.

Still on the Sound
A seasonal look at island life

Michael Faulkner

Blackstaff Press

FRONT ENDPAPER IMAGE
My parents sailing *Angelique*, a 44-foot sloop belonging to my uncle, in the early 1960s

BACK ENDPAPER IMAGE
My grandfather James Faulkner sailing *Briden* (as in 'Brian-Dennis'), a 40-foot gaff-headed
cutter, Sound of Sleat, 1932

First published in 2009 by
Blackstaff Press
4c Heron Wharf, Sydenham Business Park
Belfast BT3 9LE
with the assistance of
The Arts Council of Northern Ireland

arts
council
of Northern Ireland

Designed by Keith Connolly, Tonic Design

Printed in Italy by Sedit

A CIP catalogue record for this book is available from
the British Library

ISBN 978 0 85640 849 6

www.blackstaffpress.com
www.thebluecabin.com

To my father and mother
and
to Jock and Katie Bevan

Contents

Introduction

On a pleasant winter morning in 2007, I took the dinghy across Ringhaddy Sound and drove the three miles to Killyleagh for a working lunch at Picnic Delicatessen with Helen Wright, of Blackstaff Press.

On the table, so to speak, was a possible new writing project. A year had passed since the publication of *The Blue Cabin*, which began with our unplanned relocation in 2001 to Islandmore after the loss of my business, and consequently our home, in Scotland. My family's association with the island goes back many years. My grandfather acquired it in the 1930s, farmed it for ten years and sold it on; then my father managed to buy back just the cabin twenty years later; and when my mother, to whom the cabin passed on my father's death, offered it to Lynn and I as a base from which to take stock and move forward, we didn't have to think about it for long.

Some of my fondest childhood memories are of summer days on Islandmore in the early 1970s, and I know it was hugely important to my father, ever the family man, that during the most tumultuous years of his political career he was able to load family and dogs into a small boat and cross Ringhaddy Sound to enjoy brief – for the most part, very brief – interludes of peace and quiet at the cabin.

For many years, Lynn and I had come to Islandmore for a few days in August, but no one, as far as we were aware, had ever spent the winter there. *The Blue Cabin* chronicled our first year as full-time residents: the challenges of boat-only access, no mains electricity and a building with the insulation values of a tent; one or two close calls on the water; and the slow realisation, formed and firmed up in small but irreversible increments by the influence of this most inspirational corner of Ireland, that there is more to life than balance sheets.

Several further meetings, a draft outline and at least one more cappuccino at Picnic later, this book began to take shape. A few things, we agreed from the start. First, although to some extent a sequel, the new project should stand on its own. Also, it should be more richly illustrated. During question and answer sessions at slide shows in the year since publication, someone from the audience had invariably said, 'Have you thought of publishing your photographs?'; and I had invariably replied, without very much to go on, 'Of course.'

Another frequently asked question, 'Are you still on the island?', and the usual follow-up, 'Looking back, was it a change for the better?' provided a further requirement for the new book – that in some sense, with readers of the first one in mind, it should carry on where *The Blue Cabin* left off.

And the fourth idea, much advocated by Helen, was that rather than being simply a collection of photographs with words, for browsing, the book should have a structure – some kind of narrative progression – which invited readers to actually *read* it. So, on the basis that cabin life on an otherwise uninhabited island is shaped, more or less, by the weather, the tides and the time of year, we decided to go with the four seasons, beginning with winter.

I enjoyed that idea, if only because the change of seasons is so subjective. From the top deck of a London bus, looking down on early morning commuters, winter might be hunched shoulders, woolly scarves and a somewhat quickened pace. From the window table of a truck stop in Chilliwack, British Columbia, it might be winter tyres and snow chains. But for Lynn and I on Islandmore, winter's onset will forever be associated with one just one name: George.

From Ringdufferin, looking southwards
towards the Mournes

Winter

George

When George first introduced himself, he frightened the life out of me. It was a still, cool night in December 2007. Lynn had gone to Edinburgh to deliver paintings for the Scottish Gallery's Christmas show, so the cabin was in darkness as I approached: unusual and a little unnerving, as without some light as a point of reference, the foreshore can seem to come at you quite suddenly – out of the black, as it were. Once or twice in the past, straining to make out the jetty on a dark night and a big sea, I have met the marker pole by mistake, which may account for its slightly drunken loll in any kind of weather.

I tied up using a very quick, and quick-release, knot with the quaintly romantic name of Highwayman's or Cowboy's Hitch – depending on your taste in cultural icons – slung a bag over my shoulder, grabbed a couple of peat bales and walked carefully towards the cabin, following the pale grey lines of the plank walkway under my feet. At the very top I almost took a sideways step into oblivion when a rasping and slightly guttural grunting sound came from just a few feet away, below me and to the right. I stood very still and peered down into the darkness, half expecting the head of Strangford Lough's own *Dobhar-chu*, the Hound of the Deep, to rise silently towards me and fix me with its fiery gaze. Instead, the same sound came again; but although I still couldn't see the source, it had about it a plaintive quality that made me feel curiosity rather than alarm.

Had he been a year or two younger our terrier Rabbie, who was at my feet, would have been beside himself, but he had obviously neither heard nor scented a thing – either that or he took the intruder for a big friendly dog, and with the confidence of a home player, chose to ignore it. The two of us continued across the grass, up to the veranda and along to the front door, where I fumbled with the keys until I found one that worked, reached for the torch that always hangs behind the door on the inside, and made my way back to the jetty.

By the light of the torch, the first thing I saw was the reflection from two big eyes staring up at me from the shingle drift at the foot of the sea wall. I shone the beam to the side and knelt on the jetty for a better look. Round, fluffy, mottled and frankly adorable at such close quarters, it was a baby seal, and it wasn't about to leave just because I had turned up. On the contrary, it was sufficiently relaxed to turn its head away, and wriggle slightly from side to side, so that the shingle nest on which it was lying conformed more closely to the shape of its body. I shone the torch around, looking for an adult, but clearly it was unaccompanied: lost, abandoned – my imagination began to work overtime – perhaps sick or injured; no doubt starving . . .

Food. Water. I instinctively headed off in search of both. On my way to the fridge, which in the absence of an electricity supply to the island is a tiny gas-run caravan fridge in the generator shed behind the cabin, it dawned on me that fresh water is not something that would be available to your average seal; and also that on the food side I hadn't the faintest idea, aside from fish, what a seal – particularly a baby seal – would eat. For all I knew (later, this did in fact turn out to be the case) its last meal might have been its mother's milk. But I could think of no way to administer milk at this time of night without distressing the poor thing, and went through the contents of the fridge looking for something more substantial. What, I wondered, would *I* enjoy if I were a hungry seal pup on an unknown shore in the middle of winter? Salar's excellent hot-smoked salmon seemed ideal. I tore off a good chunk and headed back, through the gate that leads onto some stone steps to the foot of the sea wall, and crouched beside the patient. It still didn't appear in the least concerned, so I left the salmon beside its little nose, took the boat out to the mooring, rowed back to the jetty and went to bed, praying that our visitor would survive the night. Before blowing out the candle, I texted Lynn with the news, and she texted back, signing off with the typically optimistic thought that we had better come up with a name. Without

George meandering to the water on his first morning –
taken on the mobile phone

knowing whether it was a boy or a girl, or indeed whether it was a grey or a common seal, I suggested Gracie.

I slept little, and got up early. Pulling on a coat, I tiptoed to the top of the jetty and looked down. No sign; just a seal-shaped indentation in the shingle, and the salmon, exactly where I had left it. I looked around. The tide was almost fully gone, so I had a clear view of several hundred yards of foreshore on either side of the jetty. Nothing at all. Ah well, she must simply have rested up for the night, leaving on the high tide in the early hours. A good result, really, though I did feel a pang of regret that we hadn't been able to get better acquainted in daylight; and indeed, that Lynn hadn't been with me the night before.

I fed Rabbie, took toast and coffee to the window seat in the living room, and settled down to write, keeping an eye on the water for anything unusual. When I did catch a movement out of the corner of my eye, it came not from Ringhaddy Sound but from the jetty – or rather, from underneath the jetty. In no particular hurry, Gracie was making her methodical way between the timber uprights, perhaps ten or twenty yards from the sea wall. When I had gone to check earlier, she must have been directly below my feet. As I watched, she emerged from under the walkway and lolloped in a most ungainly way towards the sea, pausing every so often to look around her. I couldn't lay my hands on my camera, so the series of photos above were taken using the mobile phone. They would be the first of many.

It took Gracie a good twenty minutes to make the water, and when she did, she rolled over a couple of times in the shallows – and promptly came ashore again. By this time I was standing on the jetty, and far from being shy or suspicious now that she could see me properly for the first time, she lolloped over, looked up at me with her big black eyes and grunted in a most pathetic way, as if to say, 'Any chance of a fresh herring?'

I rang Lynn and we agreed that before rushing ashore to the fishmonger, I should call the seal rescue centre at Exploris Aquarium in Portaferry, some six miles to the south, for advice. Tania Singleton came to the phone and I explained the situation and said I would send a photograph to her mobile. She called back right away. 'He's a grey seal,' she said. (Oops.) 'About three or four weeks old. It's normal for pups to be left to fend for themselves after being weaned. When they get hungry enough, they find food for themselves. I would advise against feeding him.' (Oops again.) She added that it was unusual, though not unknown, for seal pups to turn up so close to civilisation. I explained that Islandmore is otherwise uninhabited, with boat-only access, and that Lynn and I – and Rabbie – are what passes for civilisation here, and she remarked that in that case he was a lucky pup: he would be undisturbed, but we could still keep an eye. If he lost too much condition, or stayed around too long, we should let her know – they could come and collect him, care for him and release him when he was ready.

All very reassuring. I left to collect Lynn from the airport, happy that there was no more to be done and that nature would simply take its course. By the time we returned, he would no doubt be off exploring, learning from other seals how to fish – getting on with the business of survival. On the way back to the island, having discovered that she was a he, I showed Lynn the photos and we re-christened Gracie *George*. I was looking forward to showing Lynn where he had spent the night, but was careful to downplay the chances that she would actually meet him – when it comes to animals of any kind, Lynn is a veritable Dr Dolittle – and I tried to keep my own expectations low as we crossed Ringhaddy Sound.

As we approached the jetty, not only was George still there – he actually swam out to meet us, circling the dinghy, diving, resurfacing on the other side of the jetty, and generally giving every appearance of being pleased to see us. Lynn, of course, wasted no time in getting to know him, and over the ensuing weeks, a pattern was established. Every night George would sleep at the sea wall, exactly where he had first come ashore, and every day he would kick about in the shallows or bask on the shingle, or more often, on the timber planks of the jetty itself. Lynn and he would keep up a running conversation, she sitting on the jetty and he on the foreshore below, or vice versa. Incredibly, he would allow us to step *around* him when we walked down the jetty; and when I started the outboard, I had to be very sure I knew where he was, as he developed the disconcerting habit of surfacing beside the propeller, raising his head and shoulders above the water and flapping his flippers like something out of Sea World or Disney. He very much put me in mind, in fact, of Skippy the Bush Kangaroo.

All the while, although it broke Lynn's heart, we resisted the temptation to feed him. The advice was that in the wild, so rich in nutrients is their mothers' milk, seal pups will go without food for weeks before becoming hungry enough to feed for themselves; and that to provide food, as it were, for free, would be to risk leaving them vulnerable later in their development. An adult grey seal will get through up to ten pounds of fish per day: quite a responsibility, should he ever become even partly dependent on humans in the wild.

Very logical; very hard – and we have often pondered the outcome had we succumbed.

We'll never know. In all, George stayed with us for three and a half weeks. Just before Christmas, we both had to be on the mainland for a couple of days and nights straight, and when we got back to the island he had gone. For days we kept an eye on the sound, and when he didn't appear, consoled ourselves with the thought that after so long without food, he would be out there feeding for Ireland.

But in fact he did return. I have it in my journal as 7 February. I was taking the boat out to the mooring when a young seal surfaced a couple of times near

the south entrance to the sound. Nothing unusual about that; we would see grey seals perhaps once or twice a week from the cabin, albeit normally adults and normally quite shy – typically, they surface once or twice while they progress down the sound, and then they're gone. But I called a few times, and this one swam closer. I shouted to Lynn, and she walked down the foreshore, calling as she went. I decided to stay out of it, and as Lynn stood at the lough's edge, George came into the shallows and stretched his head out of the water, turning little circles, diving and resurfacing. I suppose they chatted for ten minutes; and since that day George has done regular swim-bys, always from south to north, and always hugging the Islandmore shoreline. If we see him in time, we stop what

Top: Lynn with Shona MacDonald,
aka the seal-caller

we're doing and pass the time of day.

Most recently, George showed up while our friend Shona was staying. Lynn happened to spot him first, off Eagle Point; he surfaced briefly, then disappeared. Shona, who sings with The Trufflehunters and claims to speak fluent seal, stood on the jetty, cupped her hands to her mouth and called – a single note, long and mournful; and George surfaced by the mooring and swam in zigzags towards her, staring, fascinated; wondering, perhaps, whether someone had died. Lynn walked over, clapping her hands (which confused him, surely) and shouting encouragement; and for fifteen minutes the three of them hung out. George turned over at one point and swam on his back, bending his neck forwards to keep a weather eye on the others.

I don't know whose behaviour was more eccentric, but it wasn't George's.

Pawle Sound

Rescuing Kevin

On stormy days in winter, driving into the boat park at Ringhaddy – our departure point for the island – the only signs of human life on Ringhaddy Sound are those owners hardy enough to run the gauntlet of foam and spray on the yacht club's floating pontoons to check that their dinghies haven't flipped over, climbed up onto the walkway, filled with water, or sunk. I normally look the length of the anchorage for anything unusual: yachts adrift or aground, for example, their moorings having failed.

If I notice anything, I dig out the Ringhaddy Cruising Club members' booklet, find the appropriate phone number and break the news.

These calls are never unwelcome, however late the hour. Yachts being expensive and time of the essence, owners are apt to leave their desks or jump out of bed to mount a rescue operation, hoping to catch their investment on a rising tide, and either to tow it into deep water or climb aboard and drop an anchor before it is dumped, vulnerable and for the time being beyond reach, at the high water mark.

Sometimes I will have got there first; certainly I always try to help as best I can. But every situation is different and occasionally I have run that same gauntlet, only to stand at the outer edge of the farthest pontoon trying to decide the best response to a situation I may not properly have grasped, and feeling conspicuously irrelevant.

This happened on a foul afternoon in November. Getting out of the car, I was in two minds whether to attempt the crossing to Islandmore. A gale was blowing up the sound from the southwest and with every wave that broke over the pontoons, a sheet of spray would arch high into the air and land on the dinghies – ours included – that were corralled on the lea side. The chain of ten-metre

pontoons that form a floating 'harbour', anchored by rubberized cables to concrete weights on the seabed, was flexing and heaving against its invisible stays. Two or three people had gathered on the swinging bridge (the name at that moment was apropos) which joins the fixed to the floating section of pontoons. They were holding onto the rail, looking out across the anchorage towards the southeast, and at first I thought that something might have happened to the cabin, which lies half a mile in that general direction.

But the cabin looked safe – it was still there anyway – and bizarrely enough the only other thing I registered as I joined the little group on the bridge, was a single herring gull that flew in at low level and high speed, surfing the wind in our direction and in fact passing directly beneath our feet. Nothing better calls up a storm at sea than a gull on the run for dry land, and this one seemed blind to all else as it flared and turned, dipping in behind the stone quay a few hundred yards to the north.

Kevin Doherty on board
Harvest Home

I shouted a greeting to Wesley Stripp, who owns a business called Mayday Marine. The name is addressed more to concerned yachtsmen who wish to have their cabins valeted or their hulls polished and anti-fouled than to drowning yachtsmen who wish to be plucked from the sea; so he wasn't there in a professional capacity. He pointed towards the middle of the sound, where a relatively uncluttered fairway provides clear water through the moorings for boats that are passing from north to south, or south to north. From behind George Wright's motor cruiser *Cuan Fisher* there emerged the bow of a familiar boat, plunging and climbing, throwing out plumes of spray on both sides as it exited the fairway and entered the west anchorage, which even in November is dotted with pleasure boats of various kinds, to begin a long circle to starboard which took it between and among said pleasure boats and in the general direction of the bridge on which we were standing.

The boat was *Harvest Home,* a thirty-foot fishing boat with a small wheelhouse aft, from which Kevin Doherty worked upwards of a hundred crab and prawn pots in the lough. Kevin was leaning out through the wheelhouse door, and even at this distance it was clear that he was having trouble, because although one hand was on the wheel and he was travelling at some speed, the boat continued to follow a clockwise circle which took it once more into the fairway, and once more back among the boats; the only variation being that each successive circuit was a little wider than the last, and a little closer to the pontoons.

It was perplexing to watch. I made my way off the bridge and onto the first pontoon, and was quickly drenched. On his next pass, Kevin came close enough to make a circular motion with his free arm and to point towards the stern of the boat, and it dawned on me that he had lost steering, or at least that he could steer only to starboard. He shouted something I wasn't able to catch. I tried to read his intentions, and it seemed to me that his aim might simply be to pick up the first free mooring buoy which happened to intersect the ever-widening spiral on which he was travelling.

He swung away once more, then back again; but this time he had reduced speed and was holding a boat hook in his free hand. Clearly he wasn't going for just any mooring, but had fixed his eye on one particular buoy close in to the pontoons. He seemed to be using a combination of such steering as was available to him, variations in speed, and the paddle-wheel effect by which propellers tend to bias the forward movement of a boat: much the same method of control, and requiring as much finesse, as DC10 pilots used to employ when their tail ailerons failed and they were forced to rely on the triangular configuration of the rear-mounted engines to stay straight and level (and even, apparently, to land).

This last pass was so finely judged that I felt the vibrations through my feet as *Harvest Home* came close enough to touch. Then a final burst of speed brought her bow in line with the mooring and Kevin threw the engine into neutral, ran forward from the wheelhouse and got the boat hook round the pick-up buoy. It was quite a performance, and when the boat settled back against the mooring I could see why he had wanted to be so close to the pontoons: as usual, there was no tender tied to the stern, so presumably he wanted to minimise the chances that he would have to wait out the weather in the doubtful comfort of *Harvest Home*'s standing-room-only (and unheated) wheelhouse, by coming close enough for rescue.

Having said that, there was still a gap of twenty yards or more between *Harvest Home* and her appreciative but rather helpless audience. Someone would have to fill that gap and the person with the most appropriate boat, I could see, was me. Wesley's inflatable was probably among the other tenders tied to the pontoons, but it would be foolish to take such a light boat into such a big sea. The With, on the other hand, is fifteen feet long, famously heavy and capable of handling most conditions.

It seemed like an occasion for unthinking action so I signalled to Kevin that I would fetch the dinghy and bring him in, and while he squared away his gear I climbed aboard the With, baled a few gallons of seawater and started the outboard.

Having left from the pontoons in poor conditions many times, I'm well used to the procedure. I checked for fuel, rechecked the wind direction, cast off and allowed the boat to drift stern-first, away from the pontoons and parallel to the Ringhaddy shore; then put her into forward gear, brought her round gently and hugged the lea side of the pontoons at very slow speed and in relative shelter. Before rounding the northeastern corner and getting into rougher water, I took a wide sweep to port and brought the dinghy head-on to the wind; and then it was a matter of riding the waves as best I could and zigzagging in Kevin's general direction without shipping too much water.

Kevin was still sorting boxes and equipment on deck, and the wheelhouse door was still open, but I had no intention of waiting around for him and I continued to inch the dinghy closer to his stern. Relative to one another, *Harvest Home* and the dinghy were rising and falling a good three or four feet with every wave, and Kevin would have to choose his moment carefully. In what seemed to me like extreme slow motion, as I held the dinghy as close as possible without risking a collision, Kevin slammed the wheelhouse door on his hand, mouthed a few words which were probably not 'Thanks for coming' and vaulted neatly over the gunwale and onto the dinghy's tiny triangular foredeck, where he sat facing me with an expression of pure agony, his left hand clasped under his right armpit and the blood draining slowly from his face.

At this point, as if they weren't bad enough already, things nearly took a turn for the worse. Having picked up my cargo, I had two choices. Either I could go back the way I had come, that's to say round the outside of the pontoons; or I could follow the herring gull's example and take a shortcut under the swinging bridge, which at that state of the tide offered a clearance of perhaps four or five feet. With an extra twelve stones of ballast to keep the bow down, I decided on the latter – it would be easier, quicker and drier than going the long way round. So I allowed the bow to come round with the wind, and headed for the bridge.

I should have thought of this, but of course Kevin had his back to the bridge, was not able to read my mind and had more important things on his. Despite his weight, it was as if we were at two ends of a seesaw: as the stern slipped into the troughs, so the bow rose above the peaks, and Kevin with it. He would have to lie flat in order to be sure that 'head' wasn't added to 'hand' when the duty doctor later made a list of his injuries at the A&E department in Downpatrick. This was obvious to me, and of course to Wesley and the others standing on the bridge; but when I made up and down gestures with my arm to try to get him to duck, Kevin too made up and down gestures with his injured hand, as if to say, 'You're too bloody right it's sore!' and there came a point where I couldn't have gone astern, into the wind, even if I'd wanted to, and we were committed to the bridge for better or worse. My gesticulations became increasingly desperate and I put my free hand on top of my head and ducked down low, then pointed behind Kevin at the bridge; and whether by divine intervention or merciful instinct, he glanced over his shoulder at the last possible moment, shot me a wild-eyed look and prostrated himself on the floor of the boat.

Ringhaddy – the floating pontoons at the far
end of the walkway are obscured by spray

As we passed safely underneath, Wesley was grinning widely (with relief, I would assume) and Kevin was laughing (hysterically, I imagine); and when we got into quiet water on the other side, I tied the bow rope to a cleat on the nearest pontoon, and thought of Lord Atkin's judgment in the House of Lords in Donoghue v. Stevenson (1932), which formed the basis of the legal definition of negligence as it relates to tort (delict in Scots Law). It has always been my favourite judgment, and incidentally reconciles perfectly, in a single paragraph, the layman's view that legal prose is impenetrable, with the lawyer's that it is merely precise:

> You must take reasonable care to avoid such acts or omissions as you can reasonably foresee would be likely to cause injury to your neighbour. Who then, in law, is my neighbour? The answer seems to be – persons who are so closely and directly affected by my act that I ought reasonably to have them in contemplation as being so affected, when I am directing my mind to the acts or omissions which are called in question.

Perfect. On that very elegant definition, if Kevin's head had indeed made contact with the bridge, I would surely have been responsible. Good intentions have nothing to do with it: a stupid thing to do is a stupid thing to do. Clearly, it wasn't appropriate to raise Donoghue v. Stevenson at the time, but I felt sufficiently guilty to call Kevin later and ask about his hand. He said it was fine, that nothing was broken and that when the pain in his thumb had become too much he had used a penknife to whittle a hole through his thumbnail to relieve the swelling.

Obviously, A&E is for sissies.

Stormbound

Only in quite rare circumstances are we forced to remain on the island whether we like it or not. There has to be

1 A wind of at least gale force, which is

2 Coming from the west (i.e. from across the sound) and

3 A less than urgent need to get to the mainland – that's to say, we might stay put if one of us required urgent medical attention, but if the dog got sick we'd be off the island come hell or high water.

It only happens once or twice a year, and normally for not longer than a couple of days; but when it does it can be quite exciting. We have a little battery-run weather station in a cupboard in the living room, and a few hours before a big wind, when the drop in barometric pressure becomes sufficiently steep, it begins to beep at regular intervals in an infuriating, but admittedly quite useful, way. If we *must* get to the mainland, this is the time to do it; otherwise, there are preparations to be made. If conditions are likely to be very severe, we take the dinghy off its mooring and tie it to the lea side of the old stone quay three or four hundred yards to the north. The rowing boat, I try to protect from a battering on the jetty – which runs east–west – by carrying the stern anchor out into the shallows, away from the jetty, and either heeling it into the shingle or lodging it behind a rock.

As the cabin faces just north of west, the front wall will tend to take the brunt of a westerly wind, so anything on the veranda which is not fixed down – tables, chairs, plant pots – as well as the oil lamps and shell chimes which hang from brackets between the windows, we move into the relative shelter of the timber balustrade.

As for the cabin itself – well, it is almost a hundred years old, and having started life as a POW hut in the First World War, probably never did aspire to either comfort or permanence. It sits on stilts, so the weather comes at you from below

Ringhaddy Sound in a full-blown storm; this
photograph was taken by my uncle in February 1983.
The Blue Cabin is just visible on the far left.

as well as from the sides, and in stormy conditions the windows rattle, the tongue-and-groove panelling on the inside snaps and ripples, and the whole structure shudders alarmingly.

We were hunkered down in the living room one wild afternoon when an almighty Thwack! came from the far end of the cabin, and we rushed to the window to see a sheet of felt the size of ... well, the size of the roof of the outside bathroom, swinging violently to and fro, like a rather wilful comb-over, in front of the cabin. There was nothing to be done there and then, and eventually it came adrift, sailed over the cabin and landed in a crumpled heap on the roof of the generator shed.

Two or three days and a crash course in felting later, all was back to normal. It is one of the features of island living that just *being* there requires a certain investment of time, albeit a rewarding one in terms of acquiring new skills. If it's not the roof, it's the collapsing jetty, or a crack in the hull of the rowing boat, or a recalcitrant generator; or, worst of all, a fracture in the island's water supply pipe somewhere beneath the deceptively benign surface of Ringhaddy Sound. Always a hopeless delegator, I usually have a go myself, and in the areas of joinery, fibre glassing and Heath Robinson plumbing, that works out well enough. But inevitably, from time to time we resort to professionals, and my first question, generally, is 'Are you okay with boats?'

My old friend Allan Gray, who worked with me for many years in the furniture business in Edinburgh, when he saw me struggling at the caustic tank with an oversized Georgian front door or a butternut dresser that wouldn't stay sunk, used to offer me his assistance with the rather prescient words:

'No man is an island, Mike.'

New Year's Day

The year began with [picnic] *lunch.*

The famous first line from Peter Mayle's *A Year In Provence,* without the personal parenthetical tweak, came incongruously to mind on 1 January, when we set off by boat with our good friend and all-seasons visitor, Jessica, for a New Year's Day picnic at the north end of Islandmore.

Provençal, it certainly wasn't. The sky was full of snow, though it wasn't actually snowing, and a dusting of frost still covered the little mounds of seaweed on the foreshore. The island shivered beneath a blanket of pure white that had the characteristic gleam of a crust on the edge of a thaw. The outboard seemed unusually quiet. We puttered along looking for somewhere to land, and Lynn pointed towards a row of wooden posts, the remains of a stock fence which jutted into the sound from a tree-covered headland. Under the trees, right by the water's edge, there was an inviting-looking carpet of beech leaves and pine needles – and no snow; so I put the boat in and asked the girls to move aft so that when I hit the cut-off switch and lifted the motor clear of the water, we would be able to beach on a forgiving surface of icy seaweed and, with luck, step ashore without getting our feet wet.

I'm aware as I write this that anyone who read *The Blue Cabin,* with its scattering of landlubbers-at-sea incidents, might be saying to themselves, 'Here we go' or, in the immortal words of baseball legend Peter 'Yogi' Berra, 'It's like déjà vu, all over again'; but I can say that what happened next had nothing to do with my ability, or otherwise, to tie a sound knot. The girls did manage to step ashore with Rabbie and the picnic, and indeed I managed to follow them; but when I turned to push the boat back into the water, thanks to the dressing of frost

Jessica

on the seaweed it slid backwards a great deal faster than I had expected and the bow rope slipped between my gloved, and rather cold, fingers. For an instant I stood there contemplating the options. We were almost directly across from my uncle's house on the mainland – just a quarter of a mile – and I had a mobile phone in my pocket. One call would bring him to the rescue. But my uncle Dennis is the real-life version of the persona that I try to project myself when I'm in charge of the boat and we have a nervous guest on board – that's to say, the old sea dog who knows everything and always gets you home safe – and I wasn't sure, what with the dinghy drifting off down the lough and the three of us standing helplessly on the island foreshore within hailing distance of the mainland, that I wanted to hear his comments when he arrived on his rescue mission.

No, it would have to be a bracing winter swim. No time to discard layers – the dinghy was already in deep water and moving gently northwards on the incoming tide. I dropped the phone at my feet and waded in. By the time the water was up to my waist I felt two distinct and equally disconcerting sensations. The first, obviously, was the cold water, which quickly found its way down the inside of my boots and up the inside of my oilskin trousers; but

something else, harder to explain, was happening at the same time. I found I was unable to keep my feet, and it wasn't because I was slipping, or tripping: I can best compare the feeling to one of those dreams where immediate escape is called for, and your legs won't work. I found myself upended like a cork and spread-eagled on the surface of the water, face down, thrashing my arms and legs in a rather disorganised breaststroke and edging forwards, albeit at nothing like the speed I would expect given the effort I was expending.

For an explanation, I have to rewind five years. It is Christmas morning and the whole family is gathered in my brother David's kitchen. He has always come up with interesting Christmas presents and this time it was a two-part set of oilskins which doubles as a survival suit. The entire thing – body, legs, arms, even the hood – is lined with a highly buoyant neoprene-like material which is guaranteed to keep you afloat should you fall overboard. It has reflective tabs, a whistle for attracting attention and sundry useful-looking straps and buckles for which I will one day find a use (an ongoing project). Of course, I tried it on there and then, an operation which took some time, and I stood there next to the Aga,

feeling like Dustin Hoffman in the scene from *The Graduate* when he tries out his father's graduation present – a diving suit complete with breathing mask and oxygen, in which he can barely walk. I was twice my normal size, but I must admit I felt extremely cosy, pleasantly insulated from the outside world, and supremely, unexpectedly safe. This was a suit I could survive in for months if necessary. In the years since, no matter what the conditions outside the cabin, be it lashing rain or sub-zero temperatures, I have often managed to maintain my own climate-controlled micro-environment while rowing the punt out, starting the outboard, loading the dinghy and crossing the sound; so that by the time I have started the car, turned on the heater, eased myself behind the steering wheel and wriggled out of my cocoon, I have only really been aware of conditions by virtue of having *seen* them.

Well, I was wearing my survival suit the day we went for our picnic; but critically, only the bottom half. On a big white panel sewn into the lining of the jacket, there is a warning notice which says: *This is not a life jacket. It is a buoyancy aid only and will not self-right an unconscious person.* That may be so, but if just the

trousers are worn it turns out to be quite capable of up-ending a conscious one. The harder I struggled to 'swim' after the boat, the more determined was my survival suit that whatever happened to the rest of me, my legs would survive, so that most of my energy was going into keeping my top half on the surface.

Lynn and Jessica had heard the splash. When they saw me in the water, they correctly guessed that I was going after the boat, though of course they didn't realise I had intended to wade, and not to swim. They were more fascinated than alarmed, and simply headed back down the shore towards me, carrying the picnic basket, assuming that when it was all over the one thing we would *not* be doing was sitting down to lunch.

It probably took just a minute or two to catch up with the boat, though it seemed far longer. Once I had a hold of the bow rope, I was able to right myself, get my feet back on the stones and walk ponderously ashore, towing the boat behind. Ridiculously, and despite Lynn's protestations, I insisted on going ahead with the picnic, as we had gone to so much trouble to be there; and in the event, though it was certainly uncomfortable, my upper half, which might otherwise have stopped working, began to warm up courtesy of the central heating system wrapped around my lower. The trousers were behaving like a wet suit, allowing the water layer between skin and lining to heat up to something close to normal body temperature and no doubt sending some of that heat around the rest of me via my vascular system. This explains, as I realised later, the words *Thermotic Floatation System* on the breast pocket of the jacket. (To my knowledge, the word *thermotic* does not exist in English, but the manufacturers may have thought *thermostatic* a claim too far.)

By the time I had got a mug of coffee, two cheese and salami rolls and a raspberry and white chocolate friand inside me, I was feeling fine. We didn't dawdle over the picnic but we still had one, and back at the cabin I hung my gear in front of the wood burner to steam dry, and had one of those experiences, like sleeping late or staying in a good hotel, that have always made me feel vaguely guilty – a hot bath in the middle of the day.

The Lough's Bounty

For our first two winters we managed with a single wood-burning stove, in the corner of the living room at one end of the cabin. We depended on it for hot water as well as heat, and kept it burning – still do – twenty-four hours a day, raising the temperature on midsummer afternoons to near-sauna levels but providing some respite, at least in that one room of the cabin, during the coldest days of winter.

The temperature in the rest of the rooms, there being no insulation, more or less reflected the temperature outside: pleasant for eight months of the year, wholly unpredictable for four. We got used to layering-up; much, as my mother pointed out, like our grandparents. We finally caved in and fitted another stove in the bedroom, at the far end of the cabin, in 2003, during our second autumn. For the first time, the cabin was sandwiched between two sources of heat and it was possible to wander about during January and February wearing only jeans and a woolly jumper. Or two.

For fuel, we always keep a small amount of coal and peat under the veranda, and supplement this core stock by raiding the foreshore of Islandmore and its neighbours for flotsam and driftwood. These fuel-gathering expeditions, like our equally frequent forays for cockles and mussels on the foreshore in front of the cabin, are for me the essence of island living, and as near as I can expect to get to donning moccasins, pulling back the bear skin and stepping out through the plank door into the snowy vastness, a rifle over my shoulder and a week's supply of dried moose-meat tucked into the folds of my fur-trimmed parka.

Rabbie, as you would expect, always has a ball when we go foraging – or at the very least, a really good supply of sticks to retrieve. We cruise the nooks

Cushlin

and crannies of the island's shoreline by boat, going ashore every so often to retrieve a likely-looking limb of hawthorn (which burns with a sweet aroma), the stump of a mast or – increasingly rare these days – the remains of a wooden fish box with the name of a County Down fishing harbour stencilled in black: *Portavogie, Kilkeel, Ardglass* ... Never anything from Strangford Lough itself, which doesn't boast a fleet big enough to justify a local merchant.

The reason that this supply of quasi-natural resources never fails, has to do with geology. The greater part of Strangford Lough, geologically speaking, is in fact a flooded field, or 'swarm', of drumlins – rounded hillocks of glacial boulder clay laid down by the retreating ice at the end of the last ice age – and Islandmore, one of the larger islands in the lough, represents a cluster of these egg-shaped mounds half-drowned by the sea, the indentations between which have evolved into little bays around its shoreline: perfect traps for the occasional piece of detritus thrown up by the elements, or away by man.

There is a special satisfaction in being, or at least feeling, relatively self-sufficient in both food and heat; and rightly or wrongly I include those of the lough's resources which we have not actually had to harvest ourselves, but which come to us within hours, or even minutes, of being harvested by someone else.

Every so often Kevin Doherty, on his way past the cabin after one of his fishing trips, leaves a little something in the dinghy – always a pleasant surprise. On a late evening return journey to the island in mid-March, I found a white plastic bag on the stern seat containing something the size of a side plate, and a scrap of paper with 'KEVIN' in black letters. Kevin had recently sold *Harvest Home* but was still fishing a pretty canoe-sterned boat, *Cushlin*, for her owner.

Kevin passes by the cabin most days through the winter, and the last time I had seen him was when I got a call from John Scott, who looks after the moorings in the sound, on another late evening three weeks earlier. John told me he had had a call from Kevin, who had run out of diesel in Pawle Sound, behind Islandmore, and he asked if I could give him a tow. John would do it himself but was taking care of visitors following a bereavement. Well, I hate to pass up an adventure so despite the fact that I was three quarters of an hour away on the mainland, and hadn't intended to be at Ringhaddy till midnight, I said 'Certainly' and dropped everything. I said I wouldn't be with Kevin for an hour or more, but John said that was fine – Kevin had an anchor out and would be happy to wait. John would give him a call and tell him I was on my way.

When I got to the pontoons I left my stuff in the car, jumped into the dinghy and headed south through the moorings. I could see the lights of the cabin off to my left, and decided to land and collect a rope from the generator shed. I called ahead to Lynn, so that she wouldn't be alarmed when she heard the boat coming in; landed at the jetty and went round the side of the cabin to the shed. With a forty-foot length of polypropylene rope over my shoulder, I got back in the dinghy and continued my rescue mission.

As I left the confines of the sound, I saw a dark and indeterminate shape coming towards me, off my port bow, which materialised into two shapes separated by a rope: a little white motorboat, and the much larger *Cushlin*, under tow.

It turned out that Kevin's crew that day was a diver/chef called Martin Rafferty. To fast forward for a moment to the night of the plastic bag and its plate-sized contents, the operative word is 'chef'; but that evening it was most certainly 'diver', because unbeknownst to me, while I was speeding by car towards Ringhaddy, Martin had decided to get into his wet suit and swim ashore from *Cushlin* – not to the mainland, which was half a mile away, but to the east shore of Islandmore. Thence, an energetic hike over the top of Eagle Hill, down to the west shore opposite Ringhaddy, and another swim to Kevin's little motorboat, which was tied to a mooring in the middle of the sound. Quite a feat, and as

Kevin later said, if Lynn ever finds a calling card on the island with 'All because the lady loves', she'll know the identity of the silhouetted man in black.

So, sadly, my services were not required. I followed as far as *Cushlin*'s mooring just to see them safe, and as they were transferring their catch in boxes between the two boats, Kevin handed me a bag of razor clams by way of thanks. Curiously enough I had never tried razor clams up to that point, though we have sampled most of Strangford Lough's plentiful resources over the years. Lynn demurred, as

they are one of the few shellfish on which she's not keen, but I found them delicious – a cross, as Kevin had suggested, between squid and cockles.

Well, the mysterious plastic bag in the stern of our dinghy contained an enormous scallop shell containing the flesh of several more scallops – all cleaned and ready to cook. When I landed at the cabin I called Kevin to say thanks, and he told me that Martin recommends frying them in butter with a splash of Worcester sauce, which caramelises in the pan. We both love scallops – Lynn could live on them – so what a treat.

Since 2003 there has been a ban on dredging for scallops in the lough, primarily to protect the horse mussel communities which were threatened by it; but hand-gathering is still permitted, and we have come across Strangford scallops in eateries on both sides of the Irish Sea. When we do, bizarre though it sounds, it's with something like a sense of yearning.

Rabbie

As I write, Rab has recently turned seventeen – a good age for a Westie, but who's counting – and a couple of months ago he added the removal of his left eye to an already impressive list of surgical procedures to which he has submitted himself over the years. Well, perhaps we submitted him; but he always acquiesced, believing that even vets, to quote Gam, an old friend from Canada who took everyone as she found them, are 'just other people'. (Gam was the source of several aphorisms which have provided guidance, to a greater or lesser extent, since my teenage years, including, in descending order of usefulness: 'You're either honest or you're not, Mike'; 'Whoever they are, they're just other people'; and my personal favourite, 'There's nothing beautiful about feet'.)

Rabbie's trusting disposition, as indeed his implacable preference for human, rather than canine company, is one of his most endearing character traits. He has never enjoyed other dogs, and in fact couldn't even get along with his stable mate Jock, our cairn terrier and one year his senior, despite their spending fourteen years in the same house, the same car – even, on occasion, the same bed.

Jock passed away three years ago, and without disrespect to his immortal memory I can say that if Rabbie didn't exactly celebrate, then neither was he about to waste his time in mourning. For the first time in his life, he had us to himself, and has been able to enjoy a leisured old age without the constant need to test his position in the pecking order. That's not to say he has given up on physical activity: far from it – he doesn't swim anymore but he still intercepts and kills a football, even if he can't chase it, and his favourite toy Mousie (actually a teddy bear, but Rabbie lost the original Mousie some years ago and when we replaced him, we didn't have the heart to tell the whole truth) is never far from his side, *sans* eyes and one arm but with all other body parts intact.

There cannot exist a stronger bond between owner and dog than between Lynn and Rab. For years, they have been there for each other, have taken each other for granted. Of course, Rabbie and I love each other too; but if the two of us are walking through the trees at the side of the cabin, and he picks up a thorn, his instinct is to make a beeline for Lynn, wherever she may be, his ears laid back against his head and his tail between his legs. Lynn will scoop him up and ask him what's the matter, and he will push his nose into her ear and tell her the whole story. Only after first aid has been skilfully administered is he prepared to come and find me again – no offence, but if you're in serious need of medical attention you go to a consultant, not a house doctor.

In short, Rabbie may be the equivalent of ninety-three years of age but as far as he's concerned he's a puppy.

***

The foregoing about Rabbie, written at the end of February in a back room of the Bonham Hotel in Edinburgh, specially laid on for its direct access to the car park by a staff who were genuinely and touchingly concerned about his suddenly declining health, was overtaken by events less than forty-eight hours later. There would have been more, but because it was written while Rabbie was still with us, I felt it would do him a disservice to edit, or indeed to add to it. After all, there he was, curled up in his basket at the foot of the bed, very much a part of the team, happy to be anywhere as long as it was with us. Any additional words would have been in retrospect, and more in the nature of an obituary than a character sketch, so I'll leave it at that.

All I will say is that having gone to Edinburgh for the funeral of one much-loved friend, we ended up saying goodbye to two; and that when Rabbie decided to leave us he did so with great dignity and without having suffered.

Always a dog with a sense of humour, he even managed to make us laugh through our tears on the return trip to Ireland afterwards. We were determined to bring him back to Islandmore and to bury him near Jock (not too near – no sense in inviting confrontation); and had placed him in a cardboard box in the boot of the car, next to a couple of big drums of paint with which we intended to ensure that the Blue Cabin would live up to its name for another five years.

There was a time when you could expect your car to be inspected at Stranraer on every second or third trip; but fortunately those days are gone and apart from the obligatory, 'Are you carrying any hazardous or illegal substances?' and other standard and slightly bizarre questions, no particular interest had been shown in us at the security checkpoint, in either direction, for six or eight years.

Ironically enough that was to change on this, the only trip for which we ever *had* packed anything even vaguely doubtful. I had some recollection of notices saying, *It is unlawful to bring meat, poultry etc into Northern Ireland without authorisation from the Department of Agriculture* ... or words to that effect; and we did have some discussion on whether Rabbie was likely to fall within some sort of banned category. We hoped we wouldn't have to find out, so when I was asked at Stranraer to step out of the car and open the boot, I panicked and began rehearsing in my mind some vacuous explanations, all of which began with the words, 'I had no idea ...'; an approach which, given that any offence in this area is almost certainly statutory, liability is almost certainly strict, ignorance of the law is almost certainly no defence and I used to be a litigation lawyer, I knew, almost certainly, to be a waste of breath.

Peering into the boot, with its cargo of framed paintings, suitcases, drums of paint and a makeshift cardboard coffin, the policeman broke the ice by asking another of those checkpoint questions:

'Did you pack your car yourself?'

Sitting in the passenger seat, Lynn was staring steadfastly ahead. I tend to laugh in moments of high tension, and in order to cover up pre-emptively, I thought about saying, 'She did!' but it was hard to tell whether my uniformed friend had a sense of humour or whether that might be taken as cheek, so as seriously as I could, I replied:

'Yes.'

He nodded into the boot. 'And what is inside . . .' – it was the question we had both been dreading – '. . . the drums?'

'Ah!' I said. I happen to know quite a lot about Valtti paint – its adhesive qualities, its coverage and lifespan, the percentage of acrylic to vinyl – having used it for some years in the furniture business, and I gave him chapter and verse with some enthusiasm, while the queue of cars behind us got longer, all of us got colder and the policeman feigned interest almost to the point where I started to believe he actually *was* interested. It took only five minutes to bore him into asking me to please – *please* – close the boot and proceed to the ticket booth.

It was like *Midnight Express* without getting caught.

That incident apart, the homeward journey was horribly quiet and the arrival on the island, frankly bleak.

Next morning, we duly buried Rab on the side of the hill behind the cabin, overlooking Ringhaddy Sound. I placed Mousie beside his nose and said to him, 'Go get Mousie.' We planted daffodils above him, and Lynn found a stone on the foreshore with which to mark the spot.

The pontoons at Ringhaddy Cruising Club

Right: Ringhaddy Cruising Club

It's all me, me, me

Below: Moni
Right: With Jessica, Simon
and Namaste

With Lynn, Simon and Namaste

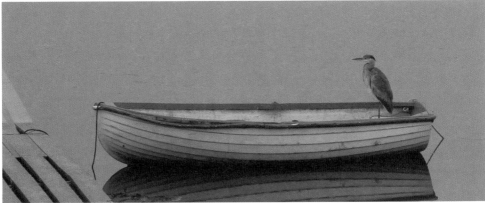

Middle: Simon and Namaste
Bottom: Dale, Lynn and Trish
Right: Pawle Sound

Spring

Eddie

After Rabbie came Eddie.

On the basis that the imposition would be unfair in their old age, Lynn decided years ago not to consider another dog while either Jock or Rab was still around; and even after Rabbie left us, I knew she would feel like a traitor even talking about it. For days, the island was a desolate place. But unbeknownst to Lynn, I had made enquiries more than a year earlier, and had a pageful of phone numbers – owners, breeders, kennels, re-homing services – in my notebook. Eventually, very tentatively, I raised the possibility of another dog.

'Spring,' I suggested, 'would be the ideal time. What do you think?'

Her response was pragmatic, but with just a hint of urgency. 'You did all right with Jock and Rab,' she said. 'Maybe you could do it again.'

My first call was to Hugh Campbell in Milnathort, Kinross-shire, from whom we had acquired Rab seventeen years before. When he answered the phone, it so took me back to the day I had collected the little chap and taken him home to Quilchena, an early Christmas present for Lynn – and to her reaction.

Yes, Hugh told me, he was still breeding; but no, he couldn't offer me a West Highland White. There was a smile in his voice, as though he couldn't wait for my next question.

'Do you have anything else?' I said.

'Would you be interested in a rare-breed pig?'

This was the first in a long list of hot leads and blind alleys, and as I followed them I gained a fair overview of Northern Ireland's West Highland terrier scene. A very agreeable bunch, every Westie enthusiast I spoke to was sympathetic to our loss and keen to tell me everything about everything, except what I wanted to hear – that they had a pup available. The ultimate collection of shaggy dog

stories. By the end of the week, we had narrowed it down to just one or two possibilities; and then I had a call from Blackstaff Press to ask me whether I would like to go on Kim Lenaghan's *This New Day* programme, on BBC Radio Ulster, to talk about island life and my forthcoming book.

When I turned up at the studio, the first question Kim asked me, off-air, was 'How's Rabbie?' She had read about him in *The Blue Cabin*, and has a famously close relationship with her own dog Ella, whom she rescued as a pup from a car park in Craigavon. When I said Rabbie had gone to the big foreshore in the sky, she said how sorry she was and that she wouldn't mention him on air. Very happy to talk about him, I said, and towards the end of the programme we got onto dogs, and of course my current mission.

This New Day must have a thoroughly invested and attentive audience, because

by the same evening there had been close to six hundred hits on my website – I was used to four or five hits a day – and my inbox was full of emails from concerned dog lovers with chin-up advice, practical suggestions and some truly heartbreaking stories of their own. The Reverend Derek Boden sent me this, by Rudyard Kipling:

Four-Feet

I have done mostly what most men do,
And pushed it out of my mind;
But I can't forget, if I wanted to,
Four-Feet trotting behind.

Day after day, the whole day through –
Wherever my road inclined –
Four-Feet said, 'I am coming with you!'
And trotted along behind.

Now I must go by some other round –
Which I shall never find –
Somewhere that does not carry the sound
Of Four-Feet trotting behind.

Suddenly, I had more leads than I knew what to do with, and the upshot was a ten-week-old Westie with an impeccable lineage and the Kennel Club-registered name of Markstown

Tartan Trews. I collected him the following Monday, and he crossed Ringhaddy Sound sitting on my lap, interested in everything, unfazed by his abduction. Lynn was standing on the jetty, and I handed him over with the unaccountable words, five months early, 'Happy Birthday, darlin'.'

She gathered him up and submitted herself to a comprehensive licking; and in that moment I knew that my caretaker role as the number one man in her life had, after two short weeks, been played out. Watching from the veranda was Lynn's mother Marion, who happened to be staying, and after she too had been introduced, she caught my attention, nodded towards Lynn and said quietly, 'Different girl'.

We wasted no time in looking for a name, though we did spend an inordinate amount finding one, eventually settling on Eddie as a name that seemed to suit him well enough, that we both liked, and that had all the right associations: 'Fast' Eddie Felson, *The Hustler*'s too-cool protagonist played by my all-time Hollywood hero Paul Newman; 'eddy', as in the state of the water; and of course ex-cop Martin Crane's show-stealing terrier Eddie, from *Frasier*. Apart from the very young, no matter who says, 'Why Eddie?' we can be sure that one or more of these will strike a chord.

For my money, the most inspiring film

Newman made was *Sometimes a Great Notion*, from the book of the same name by Ken Kesey, released in the UK as *Never Give an Inch*, about a die-hard Oregon family with a waterfront logging operation who hold out against the lumber union. But *Cool Hand Luke* runs a close second. Newman's character Luke Jackson, doing two years on a Florida chain gang for lopping the heads off parking meters with a pipe-cutter, is very much in the mould of Hank Stamper, his character in *Never Give an Inch* – both are prepared to stand alone, if necessary to die, in the face of powerful forces.

I always think of Newman when Lynn's mum comes to the island. Marion is an agile and resourceful seventy-something-year-old; but she has a weak right knee which is tested every time she steps into the boat, as a consequence of which I try to give her due warning when I come on board, or lower the motor, or in fact do anything which is likely to disturb the equilibrium of the boat while Marion is standing up. The script is always the same, and follows quite closely the opening sequence of *Cool Hand Luke*, where fellow prisoners, before moving a muscle, give the chain boss the kind of deferential notice Luke himself despises:

Takin' it off here, Boss!
Yeah, take it off, Dragline!
'Getting in the boat there, Marion.'
'All right Mike, on you go.'
Wipin' it off here, Boss!
Okay, wipe it off there, Koko.
'Puttin' down the outboard here, Marion.'
'Yes Mike, thank you.'
Drinkin' it up here, Boss.
Awright, drink it up, Gambler.
'Throwin' the rope to Lynn there, Marion.'
'Okay Mike, go ahead.'

Next day, on our first trip to the mainland with Eddie on board, to take Marion to the airport, the script simply became a little more confused.

'Can I hand you the pup, hon?'
'Okay, nice and easy.'
'Handin' Lynn the pup there Marion.'
'Okay.'
'Have you got him or have I?'
'Gettin' in the boat there, Marion. I thought you had him.'
'Thanks, that's fine.'
'I had to let him go. Can you get him?'
'Goin' after the pup there, Marion.'
'Good.'
'Where is he?'
'Under Mum's legs. Will I get the rope?'
'No, I'll give you the pup. Handin' Lynn the pup there, Marion.'
'Okay, on you go.'

You had to be there perhaps.

After Dark

Without mains electricity, much of our life in the cabin is conducted in darkness, or semi-darkness, which is something of a two-edged sword. On the one hand, we are forever feeling our way along the corridor and groping in drawers for matches, having forgotten the golden rule of cabin living – to leave a torch not far from where we might happen to find ourselves when the generator goes off; but on the other, Lynn is provided with a blank canvas on which to experiment with a range of lighting possibilities beyond imagining, using the variants of jars, bits of driftwood, sea shells, old propellers and paper bags – I'm scratching the surface – and the constant of mankind's second oldest friend, the naked flame (I sometimes mention his oldest when I meet people in the civilised world for the first time and they say, 'So, what's it like living on an island?' and I reply, rather tediously, 'Well it's the first time we've worn clothes since April.')

The most significant of these variants is the humble brown paper bag. We were introduced to *luminarias*, or if you're a stickler, *farolitos*, when we first visited New Mexico fifteen years ago, since when our friend Leslie has kept us in raw materials on her frequent trips to Albuquerque to visit family. The idea is very simple: take some flat-bottomed paper bags, pour in an inch or two of desert sand – on Islandmore, dried shingle – push a lighted candle into the sand and place inside or outside the house, in rows. At Christmas time in New Mexico, a shimmering winter blanket is thrown over the high desert landscape, and in lonely haciendas and churches, in towns, villages and distant pueblos, *luminarias* line the walkways and the streets in their tens of thousands, and adobe walls and gables are fringed with fire against the night sky.

There's no competing with that, but a person can dream. On Old Year's night, a wood fire lights up the Islandmore foreshore and we place *luminarias* at

Luminarias line the corridor at Christmas

intervals on the rail of the veranda. When friends come for dinner, we line both sides of the jetty with them. And Lynn doesn't feel constrained to confine this form of welcome to the Christmas season, or even to winter: with spring comes late evenings which are mild but still quite dark, the perfect combination for barbecues lit by Chinese lanterns, bonfires – and *luminarias*. We have even tried floating them on the water, but while the still, crisp air of Northern New Mexico may be ideal for waterborne lanterns made of bits of wood and paper bags, waveless nights on Strangford Lough, if not particularly rare, do not come to order and the spectacle of a dozen *luminarias* bobbing their way down Ringhaddy Sound, and into the open lough, is one that still awaits us.

There are other ways in which the spring air encourages us to be out and about, regardless of the light. A trip to Killyleagh, which is two miles by water, or even Portaferry (six miles) for an evening meal or to treat our guests to some live music at the Dufferin Arms or Fiddler's Green, is much less daunting in spring than in the winter months, notwithstanding that the return journey will be in the dark, with its attendant uncertainties.

On one occasion we set out for Portaferry with our friends Simon and Namaste in mild and near-perfect conditions, with dusk approaching; spent a couple of pleasant hours, and returned in driving rain and a considerable swell in the pitch dark. Someone had thought to stow a tarpaulin, which Simon pulled over his head, spreading his arms so that Lynn and Namaste could share it with him, shielding all three of them from the worst of the weather. No such luxury for the helmsman, who had to kneel on the stern locker in order to 'see' over the top of the tarpaulin, his glasses steamed on the inside, and running with rainwater and spray on the outside. This journey, travelling northwest towards Islandmore across the open lough, is very simple in daylight but requires some care after dark. There are numerous pot buoys to look out for, and a course must be set between the little island of Dunnyneil to the west and the Limestone Rocks to the east, and then along a slightly confusing line (due to the disposition of the shore lights) to the east of the Brown Rocks and the Black Rock, entering

Ringhaddy Sound from the south.

I've done it a hundred times without incident, but whether it was the distraction of the giggles and guffaws coming from under the tarp, the beam of Simon's torch which occasionally found a gap in its folds to shine directly into my eyes, or the game of I-Spy that was being conducted in clearly limiting conditions under the tarpaulin and featured an apparently hilarious number of 'Something beginning with "S"s', and 'Something beginning with "W"s', I don't know; but I managed, having successfully left Dunnyneil, the Limestones and quite a number of barely visible buoys behind, to wander off course on the final leg by confusing the lights of the boathouse on Simmy Island with those of the Stringers' house on Ringhaddy Sound. I ended up *inside* the Brown Rocks and perilously close to the boulders spreading out from Ringdufferin Point, which are below the surface of the water but not so far as to give sufficient clearance for a long-shafted outboard (like ours) at this stage of an ebb tide.

Can you see the far shore from your window?
Are the moorings in shadow or light?
Is the gleam in your eye from the western sky –
Is it still on the sound tonight?

Having realised something was wrong, but not yet aware exactly where we were, I startled the others by throttling down to idle speed, cutting the motor and asking for the torch. I always pack the Admiralty chart of Strangford Lough when we are away from base, and I unfolded it on the vacant seat in front of me and peered to left and right of the boat, looking for some recognisable landmark. Having found one in the shape of the all-too-close pine trees on Ringdufferin Point, I made my apologies and used the depth markings on the chart to exit the passage between the Brown Rocks and the mainland, going back the way we had come and taking a long sweep *outside* the rocks to regain command of the situation and, hopefully, some of my pride.

I know that Lynn will have tied another mental knot in the drawstring of her virtual life jacket: *Do not return from Portaferry after dark.* This will be beside the one that warns *Do not go to Portaferry in a strong wind,* the background to which is well-rehearsed in *The Blue Cabin* and involved one of our very few life-threatening experiences since coming to the island. A gentle swell turned so quickly into a big sea that we almost swamped the dinghy, and I'm sorry to say that Lynn's happy-go-lucky attitude to small boats changed forever.

Three strikes and you're out: it's only a matter of time before she adds a third knot – *Do not go to Portaferry. Full stop.*

It may be foolish to record these things. One of Lynn's oldest friends, who lives in Colorado, emailed us after *The Blue Cabin* came out, saying how much she enjoyed it and how she looked forward to her first visit to Islandmore. Terrific, we said, can we fix something up? – to which Judy rather ungraciously replied:

'Will Mike be driving the boat?'

The Boat Season

Through the winter, from our vantage point at the south entrance to the sound, days or even weeks go by when the only things moving on the water are the two resident fishing boats, the odd early morning winkler or wildfowler – and us. Most of the yachts have been hauled out and lined up in tidy rows in the boat park for the down season. Come April, however, having supervised the haul-out six months earlier with heavy hearts – 'That's it for another season' – owners show up at the boat park with long-handled rollers, cans of anti-fouling and big grins, and the club skip fills up with intriguingly varied and colourful cardboard boxes, like the day after Christmas. *Micro-deluxe gimballed cabin heater (brass). Go-sea Mk II Sat-nav 1014. Blivits, marine, stainless, (ass'td).* While his boat is 'on the hard', ask any yachtsman what he's up to and the answer will always be the same: 'Just pottering'.

Truth is, they can't wait to get on the water. Urgent calls are made to resident boatman, shipwright and can-do man John Scott, for moorings to be lifted and serviced, if necessary replaced, and during the weeks leading up to launch-out in May, John's barge can be seen in the sound most days, moving like a drone bee from one mooring to the next. A single mooring can take half an hour or half a day, depending on wind conditions and how much chain, how many shackles and swivels and so on require replacement. Typically, mooring chains last from one to three seasons, and exactly when to replace them can be a matter of fine judgement. For obvious reasons, John will err on the side of caution, albeit the job will necessarily take longer and galvanized chain and good shackles are relatively expensive. If the owner is involved at this point, a little verbal dance can take place involving the variables of cost, condition and above all, responsibility. I have been on the edge of one or two of these exchanges, which go something like this:

'Doesn't look too bad to me John.' *No sense in throwing money away.*

'Well, the links at the bottom end are a bit thin. You might get another season out of it, but it's up to you.' *I'm the one that will get the telephone call (and the blame) if the boat ends up on the rocks . . .*

'Maybe we should leave it one more season, what do you think?' *If John says it'll do, it'll do.*

'Well, as I say the links at the bottom end are that bit thin, but it's up to you.' *. . . at 3 a.m. on a Sunday.*

'Go on then, let's replace the whole thing.' *I love my boat.*

'I would say that's wise.' *Good call.*

Both parties to this delicate negotiation know that in the event of a wrong decision, it's no use invoking third parties – saboteurs, the weather, the will of God. A failed mooring is a failed mooring. Nothing – not even the facts of the case of McLeod v. Glasgow Corporation which explored the principle forty years ago, when a member of the public sued Glasgow Corporation for negligence when he gave himself a nasty injury sitting on a public convenience which shattered under his weight (later eliciting from him the immortally understated evidence in court that he felt 'a wee jag') – better illustrates the legal principle of *res ipsa loquitur* – the thing speaks for itself – than a failed mooring.

The penalty for a wrong decision is at the discretion of the gods, who on at least two occasions that I can remember, must have been smiling. Just after dawn on a windless morning in April, our friend Sean was walking along the veranda to the bathroom. He was admiring the view, which at that moment included the curiosity of a yacht, *Run Na Mara*, lying unusually close to the cabin, off the perpendicular and, if his half-closed eyes weren't deceiving him, on top of the jetty. She seemed so peaceful and at home, apparently he hesitated and took a few moments to look at the logical possibilities before saying to himself, *This can't be right,* and waking us up. Sean's wife Christine and their little girl Erin, on her first island adventure, watched with Lynn from the living room window while

Sean clambered aboard the yacht from the jetty and I went for the dinghy. We fixed a line to her bow and towed her into deep water, tying up to the nearest vacant mooring before heading back for a couple of hours sleep, another salvage operation successfully and painlessly completed.

On the other occasion, it wasn't that something had appeared in the wrong place but that it was missing entirely, and embarrassingly enough neither Lynn nor I spotted its absence. All year long, the most obvious feature in the sound is the Monsons' converted trawler, *Family's Pride* – fifty-two feet long, bright red and lying directly across from the cabin. Hard to miss, you would think. Well, we got up one morning, stoked the wood burners, had breakfast overlooking the sound and went our separate ways, Lynn to her studio and me to one of the back bedrooms which doubles as an office. Only later, when John Scott motored past the cabin and returned in half an hour with *Family's Pride* under tow, did the penny drop. It seems she had drifted, under cover of darkness, round the south end of Islandmore and into Pawle Sound, where she lay patiently in deep water, like a sheep in a thicket, and waited for rescue. *Family's Pride* intact, ours somewhat dented.

Since then, when I check the anchorage over, day or night and particularly after bad weather, to the usual suspects of *dragged, aground* or *awash* I have added *gone for no apparent reason*. Recently, I heard James Mawhinney's fishing boat passing by the island in the early morning. Later, I left for the mainland myself, returned at dusk and noticed that he wasn't on his mooring to the north of the pontoons. This struck me as odd because although we wouldn't always see him on both his outward and homeward journeys – he often re-enters the sound from the north – he would normally be back, one way or another, by mid-afternoon. It was blowing quite hard from the southeast, so I knew that out in the lough proper there would be a good sea. When I got to the cabin I used the binoculars to check again. Still no sign; but it's possible to miss a boat at that range and in poor light, so I called my uncle at the north end of the sound. As far as he was aware, James hadn't passed in either direction that day. He said he would call

Sail-pasts at Ringhaddy Cruising Club are reserved for special occasions – this one was in 2004.

John Scott and see if he knew anything about James's movements. Foolishly, I mentioned that I had left the dinghy tied up to the jetty, just in case 'for any reason' it might be needed later, to which he very sensibly said, 'On no account take the dinghy on the lough in these conditions. That's what the Coast Guard is for.'

One phone call led to another, and eventually to the crane operator contracted by James to lift his boat out at Killyleagh, for normal maintenance, that afternoon. My uncle called to tell me; which saved me lying awake that night, turning it over and over in my mind, jumping out of bed at two in the morning and saying to Lynn, 'I'll just pop round and see if I can see him.'

Fuss fuss – but you can't be too careful.

It's worth saying, that doing a Brian Hanrahan and counting them all out, counting them all in, is all very well in wintertime, when there are so few boat movements on the sound. But come May, when the moorings are all occupied, the days are longer and warmer and Strangford Lough reverts to its summer persona as the ultimate day-sailor's playground, this would be a practical impossibility. On a sunny Sunday afternoon, departing from the jetty is like stepping off the pavement – *port, starboard, port again* – and the view from the veranda, if you're into boats, is a veritable ... I was going to say 'beauty' parade, but boats do come in all shapes and sizes. We have our favourites, of course. Frank Petticrew's *Magdaleyne*, a Nicholson 43, the prettiest yacht in the anchorage, is always a pleasure to watch; likewise *Dundrum*, built by McGruer's of Helensburgh in 1966 (who also built the very fetching *Ptarmigan*, my brother David's last boat); and we have come to expect a blast from the ship's whistle when George Wright passes by in his motor cruiser, *Cuan Fisher*.

Come dusk, our waving arms begin to ache, but as they say, it's a good ache.

Left: From Long Sheelah looking south

On Dunsey Rock

Richard and Johnny Moore, second cousins Anna and Alex,
and the usual sprinkling of Hawkins

Breakfast

Just as sandwiches taste better on a mountainside, it's hard to beat the foreshore for fried eggs, pancakes, hash browns, crispy bacon and maple syrup; or the chile-head's alternative of *huevos rancheros* (for which, see the recipe at the end of this chapter). Most of our guests have been treated to one or other of Lynn's classic island brunches at some time or another, and the hotter the morning sun and the lower the tide, the further we migrate from the cabin to enjoy it.

These days, of course, pancakes and maple syrup as a combination is ubiquitous, but for the real thing, with grits and hash browns, home-made waffles and eggs over easy or sunny-side up, you still have to cross either the Atlantic, or Ringhaddy Sound. If the former, we can recommend the timber-built Eagle Café, on Pier 39 in San Francisco, where they have been serving enormous breakfasts since 1928, and from which you can admire the hundreds of sea lions hauled out on floating pontoons in the bay below. We can't compete with that, but there's always George.

Twice in recent years, for the twenty-first birthday celebrations of my second cousins Anna and Alexander respectively, our cabin has been the morning-after breakfast venue for a dozen very convivial partygoers, who after a spectacular dinner under the stars in the ruins of Ringhaddy Castle, have spent the night in spartan conditions at the north end of the island, and honed their appetites by walking along the foreshore to the cabin. Most take to the water before breakfast, and then collectively we consume enough *huevos con tocino* on the veranda – my thanks to Robert Service, the poet, for a typically apropos expression – to shame a healthy hog.

It's one of the sublime benefits of being married to someone as ageless as Lynn that we can manage to relax in the company of people a generation

Jock and Pam

removed in either direction. As you would expect for a twenty-first birthday, most of this particular crowd would be in their early twenties; but looking in the other direction I can honestly say that we have never shared more exciting adventures, or laughed as much, than when two of our oldest and dearest friends came to the island for an early spring visit in 2007. Jock and Pam were both in their eighties, and if I were to wish for anything for myself in later years it would be a generous dose of their inspirational life-view.

If we opt for an off-island breakfast, there are two choices: a bacon roll picnic on any one of a dozen small islands within fifteen minutes by boat; or, since 2003, Picnic Delicatessen and Café in Killyleagh, where the morning specialities include bagels with scrambled egg and Bayonne ham, and porridge with chopped bananas and maple syrup. Unless the weather is atrocious, we go to Killyleagh

by boat, tying up at the only section of the original working harbour that still exists, where the Dibney River flows under Shore Street and into the bay. Sadly, some years ago the waterfront at Killyleagh shared the fate of its counterpart in Dundrum, fifteen miles to the south: both were built upon for, and indeed lost to, private housing developments which have been taken right to the water's edge, so that these days it's possible to drive around either of these essentially seaside villages without being aware that you are beside the sea.

When Lynn's sister Fiona and her husband Geoff last came to stay, we set off for Killyleagh one morning with high expectations and empty stomachs, planning to tie up at the harbour wall as usual. Lynn did make the comment before we left, that the tide was almost fully out, and still falling; and I said that I thought the steel ladder went all the way to the base of the harbour wall at Killyleagh, and that as long as we stuck to the river channel we would be able to take the boat all the way in.

Fortunately, Fiona and Geoff enjoy the water and are unfazed by, well, sticky situations. Likewise the kids. Roy, at that time, was eleven and Tammy nine. The two of them had already spent an entire day 'fishing' for crabs from the jetty, using limpets, lengths of string, a bucket half-filled with seawater and of course their native wits. They had been given the options of a holiday in the sun or on Islandmore, and had gone for the island – a great compliment. We owed them. We said that breakfast would be an adventure and en route to Killyleagh they each had a shot at the helm – Tammy cautious and ladylike, watching her speed; Roy a little more gung-ho and watching his too, but for different reasons.

On the approach to Killyleagh, it's important to keep the brick tower to the west if you want to stay in deep water; and to pass through the actual anchorage, with its cluster of boats and moorings, for the same reason. For this bit, I retrieved the helm from Roy, and began looking for the channel which would take us all the way in to the harbour wall; but I have to say that as channels go, it wasn't all that obvious. I asked Roy to go forward and to call out the depth, throttled back to idle speed and raised the outboard so that the propeller was just below the

The lower the tide, the further we migrate from the cabin

water – a nifty, if rather noisy trick which always attracts the attention of anyone within a quarter of a mile of the boat.

At that time (10.30 on a Saturday morning) the only people who were within a quarter of a mile of the boat were an elderly couple walking along the narrow pathway between the aforementioned housing development and the edge of the harbour. They waved, and although things were already taking an embarrassing turn, I waved back, with as much languor as I could muster. I thought of Bill Bryson, and his description in *Down Under*, grizzly and compelling in equal measure, of a human arm regurgitated by a fourteen-foot beige shark in front of horrified spectators at an aquarium in Coogee, Australia. Bryson had recently been instructed in the correct procedure to follow when you are swimming, and find yourself with an unwelcome chaperone – black, shiny, and more or less triangular. Apparently the drill is to face the shore and wave one arm 'languidly', which of course he assumed to have been the last voluntary action of this particular arm . . .

If there ever was a channel, we were unable to find it. At first, Roy called out the depth with calm efficiency, but as we came closer to the harbour wall, each call acquired an added note of urgency and a few more decibels:

'Two feet six . . .'

'Two feet . . .'

'Eighteen inches!'

'EIGHTEEN INCHES!'

Our audience of two had taken their seats ringside, on a bench at the neck of the harbour, and were politely looking around with bored expressions at everything except us.

I lifted the motor out of the water entirely and suggested we pole the rest of the way in. Geoff went to the bow with one oar while I stood in the stern, and between the two of us we inched the boat closer to shore. It wasn't easy to stay on task, or indeed not to laugh, because there was nothing to push on but mud, and as all school children with interesting science teachers know, every action has an equal and opposite reaction. The amount of effort that went into each new push was only marginally greater than the amount required to extract the oar from the mud afterwards, so that 'inched' quickly became the operative word.

(My own science teacher from the age of eight to twelve, Bolo, was exceptionally interesting. For the annual school riding display, choreographed by Albert Uprichard and starring half a dozen shaggy ponies and the members of the riding club, costumed, painted and full of reckless enthusiasm, Bolo used to stuff gunpowder – I can tell you the exact recipe to this day – into old exercise books rolled up very tight and bound with wire, and fit these with detonators controlled by wires stretching to the nearest tree, so that for The Charge of the Light Brigade he contrived so impenetrable a wall of fire and smoke for us to gallop headlong into, that the shrieks of watching parents had as much to do with fear as appreciation. Into the mouth of hell rode the six.)

Inevitably (with hindsight), the dinghy ground, slid – squelched – to a gradual halt. The audience perked up right away, our predicament now so obvious that no one could have expected them to ignore us any longer. They smiled and pointed and gave us the thumbs up, and when I cupped my hands and shouted, 'Any chance of a sandwich, it might be a long wait!' they rocked with laughter, smiled, pointed, gave the thumbs up again. After perhaps ten minutes of fruitless flailing and splashing and a creditable amount of self-control, Geoff and I had to admit defeat, and put down the oars. The six of us sat there in silence while I studied the tide tables, looked at my watch, and stared at the tide line to see whether it was moving, and if so in what direction (very difficult when there was nothing there but featureless mud). Finally Lynn said quietly, 'I'm watching a stone', which of course the kids found hilarious; but in fact it was Lynn's intent five-minute examination of a small stone at the edge of the water which told us for sure that the tide had turned, and was on the flood. Excellent. The wait wouldn't be as long as I had feared – not nearly long enough for a real crowd to gather.

Within twenty minutes the keel lifted clear of the mud. We conferred very briefly on whether to give it another half-hour and try again for the harbour wall; but decided that our chances of having breakfast before lunchtime were higher if we retreated to deeper water, and motored to the south side of the bay, and the pontoons of Killyleagh Yacht Club. We waved goodbye to the elderly couple, who were wandering off, the show over; and once arrived at the yacht club, we explained our situation to the only person around, who seemed to know everything about everything. He showed us where to tie up the boat, and we said we were off for breakfast, and would only be an hour. He told us he planned to be around for at least an hour himself, showed us to the gate and said he would leave it off the latch for our return. Meantime he would keep an eye on the boat. What a helpful chap; I didn't get his name and have been intending to pop back and find him, thank him for his hospitality.

By the time we got to Picnic it was already beginning to busy up for the lunchtime crowd, which Roy, bless him, saw as a marketing opportunity for my book. John and Kath, who own this small but perfectly formed café below the fairytale turrets of Killyleagh Castle, have been good enough to stock *The Blue Cabin* since it was first published. Roy fetched a copy from the counter as we were finishing our second round of cappuccinos and milkshakes; sat down, leaned towards me and said, in confidential tones: 'What if I was to go round the tables, show them the book and tell them it was written by my uncle, who happens to be sitting over there, and will probably write something in it and sign it for you, if you buy a copy?' And he would have done it – he was itching to do it – if I hadn't chickened out on his behalf, a succession of imagined Thank-you we're fines, and Not today thank-yous already making me blush.

For the record, and in case John and Kath would welcome one more for the breakfast menu:

Huevos Rancheros

We first encountered this Mexican classic in Café Pasquale, Santa Fe, New Mexico twelve years ago. On signboards outside some of the eateries on and around the plaza in downtown Santa Fe, the relative heat of the current pick of green and red chiles would be scrawled in chalk: *Moderate. Hot. Wow!* It varied on a day-to-day basis, so if you were in need of a chile hit – and we always were – you made a note and ordered appropriately.

This is how Lynn serves *huevos rancheros*, but there are numerous variations:

Ingredients

eggs
corn tortillas
pinto beans
fresh coriander
limes
salt and pepper
green or red chile sauce

Fry two eggs.

Heat a corn tortilla in a skillet or a dry hot pan, preferably cast iron, for a few moments – not long enough to crisp.

Place the tortilla on a plate with refried beans on the side (pinto beans soaked overnight, cooked and then mashed with chopped coriander, a squeeze of lime, and salt and pepper; canned refried beans work just as well).

Now, place the eggs on the tortilla and top with a generous quantity of green or red chile sauce. We use homemade tomato salsa with a teaspoon of chipotle chile added (Lynn's chipotle recipe is on page 188 of *The Blue Cabin*), but you get the more traditional red or green chile sauce from Mexican food importers.

Add fresh coriander and a squeeze of lime to serve.

Above: (from left) Jamie,
Lucinda, Rory, Lynn, Gail,
me, Claire and David
Left:Niall
Opposite: Ringhaddy Sound

On board the *Fisherboat* c.1973

Top: Rory, Lucinda and Jamie
Middle: John Scott

Summer

West Shore, Pittenweem, Fife

Off-Island

Lynn's professional life as an artist is punctuated by deadlines: to complete one or two pieces far enough in advance of an exhibition to provide publicity images; to produce a body of work for the show itself; to hand in at the gallery, collect unsold paintings, and so on. Intense pressure and brief lulls, in waves. When we lived in Scotland this wasn't a logistical problem – almost all of Lynn's exhibitions are in Scottish galleries – though it may have been a psychological one; but now that we live on an island on the other side of the Irish Sea, meeting these deadlines can be fraught.

The lengthening days of early summer are the most intense of all. Lynn's little studio by the water's edge becomes a no-go area, sometimes even to Eddie. When the air is still, the only sound is the occasional rumble of castors on the wooden floor as she turns a painting around, working it up until the composition comes together to her satisfaction. If she does emerge in her paint-spattered apron (which, having all the colours in her palette, I often think would make an interesting piece, cut to a rectangle and framed), it's normally to take a few backward steps on the timber deck, her eyes always on the work; Eddie and I glance at each other and back at Lynn, but she's gone and might not reappear for hours, lost in the studio that time forgot.

And all because one annual fixture, by virtue of the sheer volume of work required, looms larger than any other. For ten years now Lynn has shown at Pittenweem Arts Festival, in the East Neuk of Fife. During the first week of August, this normally tranquil little fishing village comes spectacularly to life as every school room, garden shed, net loft, nook and cranny is taken over by local or visiting artists, and upwards of thirty thousand visitors browse a hundred venues, wandering the steeply twisting wynds from which views of the Firth of Forth are

Islands At Low Tide 61x61cm
Lynn McGregor RSW

Autumn Spray 61x61cm
www.lynnmcgregor.co.uk

133

framed by gaps between the pantile roofs and stepped gable ends so characteristic of this part of Scotland.

Lynn shows her work on the harbour front, in a meeting room on the top floor of the Harbour Master's Office, next to the fish market – a good venue, as Pittenweem is one of the few harbours on the east coast of Scotland that still boasts a fishing fleet, and the market is still the beating heart of the village.

First, though, we have to get there. We tend to leave the island a week before the festival, to allow time for framing and for organising the venue. As the departure date approaches, Lynn's normally mellow disposition becomes, can I say, less relaxed; partly because inevitably we will have delayed photographing the work until the last minute – Lynn's paintings, by the measure of a set of benchmarks known only to herself, are works in progress until the moment I wrest them from her hands, put them on an easel at one end of the veranda, set the colour balance on the camera, say 'still please' and press the shutter release – but also because we both know that when the time comes, if conditions on Ringhaddy Sound are choppy, rainy, or both, there is a good chance that paintings will be marked and therefore unframable.

For my part, I pray, which every July up to and including 2007, seems to have worked. This time, though, as I left the jetty under a grey sky, with the first batch of boards stacked on the seats of the dinghy in neat piles three-up, foam-wrap between each board, I noticed one or two specks appearing on the back of the topmost paintings, looked skywards and panicked. It was too late to turn back so I throttled up and continued towards Ringhaddy; but that simply added a scattering of larger, saltier marks to the ones already there, so I eased off and clambered forward, taking off my coat and jumper and placing them over the two piles closest to me. By the time I had arrived at the slipway and gone for the car, a spot of rain had turned into an out and out downpour, and as I lifted the boards out of the boat, wiped off the worst of the water with a sponge, and stacked them in temporary piles on the passenger and back seats, I could feel a burning sensation on the back of my neck from the binoculars which I knew Lynn would have brought to bear as the only means of getting closer to the imperilled fruits of almost six months of concentrated labour.

On close inspection, there was indeed some marking on the painted sides, but it was confined to the edges and would be hidden by the frames, so we got away with it. The shower had passed by the time we crossed with the second batch of paintings and our luggage, and we made the meaningless resolution, not for the first time, that in future the work should cross a day early.

On the ferry to Troon, as always when we travel to Scotland, there was a sense of homecoming. Lynn was born in Fife and trained in Edinburgh; her mother lives in Pittenweem; I went to Scotland to qualify as a solicitor and stayed on; and for ten years after we married, we lived in semi-isolated contentedness in a converted farmhouse in Kinross-shire. Islandmore is a beautiful and inspiring place to live, but we did not quit Scotland by choice and will probably return there – eventually, I should think, for good.

After an overnight stay in Edinburgh, where we enjoyed feeling like tourists in our adopted city, we delivered the paintings to Perth for framing, and as they wouldn't be ready for two days, took the opportunity to travel northwest, to the wild and rugged Trossachs, and a place which holds a special significance. Lynn is a McGregor and this is Rob Roy country, but as I can't think of anyone less tribal in their outlook, the association, for her, is quirky but incidental, the strongest ties here being of an altogether less historical, and more personal nature. As we left the main road at Balquhidder and followed the single track deep into the hills, she let out the fifteen-minute, five-mile long, inward equivalent of a deep sigh, and began to relax in a way that doesn't seem to happen anywhere else. Thickly wooded slopes rose sharply away to the right, and on the left the rocky shores of Loch Voil came to within a few feet of the road. Our ultimate destination – come to think of it, in many ways *the* ultimate destination – was Monachyle Mhor Hotel, a converted farmhouse and steading which somehow manages to combine seclusion and romance with full-on, contemporary luxury and world-class dining; but as always, we paused en route at a point where the road takes a tight loop around the edge of a shingle bay, and a heroically tenacious Scots pine seems to grow, without any obvious means of sustenance, directly out of a rocky outcrop at the water's edge.

Lynn's parents used to come here. Her father painted several watercolours of the loch, including the tree on the rock; and when he died twelve years ago, we scattered his ashes at its base, establishing a permanent link that has been a source of comfort and peace for Lynn ever since, and especially since leaving Scotland.

We managed a night in Monachyle Mhor and then travelled further north and west to the equally beautiful, even more wild and rugged west coast, and Ardfern, in Argyll. To our great good fortune, Ardfern has been comprehensively colonised during the last twenty years by various branches of the Bevan family, originally from Fife and collectively our oldest and dearest friends, so we go there as often as we can. Lynn always comes away replete with inspiration, and it's no accident that the titles of her paintings – *Strangford Shores, Fife Fields, By Loch Doine, Hills (Argyll)* – have a common thread, braided by fours, blues predominating.

The tree on the rock, Loch Voil, Perthshire

Ardfern, Argyll

Crumble at Monachyle Mhor Hotel, near Balquhidder

We stayed a day and a night in Ardfern and returned to Perth for the paintings; thence to Pittenweem. This is always an exciting moment (perhaps attended by a modest rise in the artist's blood pressure): it is the first time we have seen the paintings all together in their frames, and the point from which Lynn begins to look seriously ahead at the best groups and combinations for the tricky business of hanging. Proper presentation is important to her, and she is good at it, having learned the subtle art of hanging a show from her former tutor Bill Gillon, the wonderfully talented Edinburgh artist to whom, incidentally, she owes much else besides. Lynn's landscapes may be heavily abstracted, but (don't tell anyone) she is more than capable – along, I should think, with most good abstract artists – of producing exquisite representational drawings and paintings

The Edinburgh skyline from the roof of the Bonham Hotel

from life, and the foundations of that skill were laid in Bill Gillon's life drawing classes.

From here on, I'm in a supporting role and do as I'm told. It takes two days to clear the room, install the lighting and hang the exhibition. Then there is a preview night before the festival finally opens to the public – normally on the first Saturday of August – and Lynn settles down to a gruelling week of doing something from which the gallery system normally insulates her: standing in front of her own work, fielding questions about working methods, inspirations, materials, and the really difficult what and why questions – 'What is that shape there?'; 'Why did you decide to put the horizon line there?' Her best work being informed as much by the subconscious as the reasoning side of her brain, questions like these can force her to rationalise a painting in a way that would have been distracting, even destructive, during the creative process.

Her venue overlooks a loading area in front of the fish market and this year, on the afternoon of the first day, a private coach pulled up and half a dozen women of a certain age emerged, notebooks in hand. They bunched up to listen to the only one in the group who wasn't carrying a notebook, and then headed off in six different directions. One of them, a pleasant woman in an exuberantly patterned summer dress, appeared minutes later in Lynn's space, glanced at her notes and said, 'Do you work in acrylic or oil?'; to which Lynn replied, 'Acrylic'. A lengthy interview followed, and when it was over the woman bought a festival catalogue, asked Lynn if she wouldn't mind circling those venues she particularly recommended, and went off with a smile on her face and a spring in her step.

She must have passed one of her classmates on the stairs, because another equally enthusiastic woman appeared at the door, took in the four walls with a single sweep, glanced at her notes and said, 'Do you work with acrylics or oils?'

In all, we are off the island for a little over a fortnight, but our Scottish itinerary – Edinburgh to Balquhidder to Ardfern to Pittenweem – reflects a need within both of us which was largely born of, and shaped by Islandmore: the need to be by the water.

John and (my godson) Harry Hawkins

The Two Johns

I was halfway to the mainland one morning, a little out of sorts, when my mobile chirped. I cut the outboard and drifted; and as I read John Hawkins's text I began to smile, and then to laugh. Incidentally John is one of the few people I know (Lynn is another) who never texts in txt spk.

> Good morning Mr Mike. I was sitting at Stansted waiting for a flight and thought of you both. I hope all is well. I had some frozen velvet crabs for dinner last night. Lidl's best. It's not quite the same when you don't have to engage in the primeval, visceral struggle to put them in the pan. Frankly, they were a bit of a disappointment. I trust the artist is daubing away in her studio and that The Blue Cabin II is coming along. I've a nasty suspicion that the 'unable to remain upright on the jetty' and 'fishing for watch by torchlight with a deactivated magnet' scenarios may not show me in a favourable light if they come to print. Please delay or exercise artistic licence. Much love to you both. John

Well if that's not an invitation I don't know what is.

> Good morning to you too John. Very good to hear from you and especially good to think of you heading in that direction [the Hawkins have a place in France] … Apropos the velvets, I might just quote you on that because what better image than JH sitting in Stansted Airport, dreaming of heroic

battles with the monsters of the deep? Excellent. As far as the jetty and the expensive timepiece go, I feel a rewrite coming on, or at least a new introductory paragraph: 'When our OTHER Hawkins friends came to stay . . .' Actually, I'm sure you know that the more you protest professional sensibilities, the more you open yourself to ridicule. See you in court. Have a safe journey. Mike

To be fair, the watch debacle wasn't like John at all. By nature he is quite a sensible, cautious fellow, like myself – not given to slapstick or risk-taking. By way of example, during this particular visit I had to be off the island for a day to do a book festival reading, and returned after dark. The arrangement was for John to bring the dinghy to collect me from the pontoons. I called when I was still ten minutes away, so that he would have lots of time to get in the boat and cross the sound. When I arrived at the boat park and turned off the headlights, I was able to make out the glow from the cabin living room in the distance; but the sound was otherwise in darkness. No doubt John, and possibly Sam, or even all four of the Hawkins boys, would at that moment be weaving their capable way through the moorings, heeding my advice to use their peripheral vision, to look up and to the side, never straight ahead. Shortly they would emerge from the darkness and come alongside the outer pontoon, on which I decided to station myself – hungry, a little washed out, and eager to hear about the day's events; in particular, about the fish tally.

Then I saw a single, brighter light. It was moving away from the cabin, downwards and a little to the right, which meant that someone was on the jetty. The light stopped; bobbed about, dropped suddenly; bobbed about again. Then it was on the move, and coming my way. So much for my advice about night vision – evidently John had decided, like many others at Ringhaddy, in all fairness, who use torches to light the way to their yachts, that the Apache way was for the Apache, to whom the directional beam was not historically available.

John and Sam make the pontoons after a long sea crossing . . .

I waited and watched. The light disappeared behind a black silhouette that I knew, from its position, to be the yacht *Lady Shamrock*, close to the Islandmore shoreline. It reappeared briefly some time later, only to disappear again almost immediately behind another cluster of boats, a little – a very little – to the north. Minutes passed. I looked at my watch and paced the pontoons, stopping every so often to peer into the darkness. Still no sign. Minutes turned to hours and at last, in the first grey light of early dawn . . . No, they did in due course arrive at the pontoons, John and Sam together; it just took longer than usual. While Sam had steered the boat, his father had, literally, blazed a trail from his position in the bow. This procedure works well enough, but the compass of one's visible world is redrawn to a radius of ten or twelve feet from the boat, almost everything further out being, for practical purposes, invisible. Thank goodness for the flashing red light on the end of the pontoons – it must have been an invaluable beacon during the long sea crossing. I took a photograph as they arrived, in which Sam's eyes are closed, suggesting he might have been sleepwalking: not surprising given the epic nature of the voyage. His father, torch in hand, has the look of a Knox-Johnston after three hundred and twelve days of single-handed circumnavigation – elated, perhaps unsure of his land legs but relieved to have made land at all.

Now, when our *other* Hawkins friends came to stay . . .

Curiously enough, the patriarch of this other Hawkins family is also a John, and he too has three sons named Sam, Tom and Harry. To cap it all, both Johns have wives called Emma. Well, this other John Hawkins brought with him a pair of Barbour wellingtons which were excellent in all respects (I should know, since he left them behind) except that the soles were designed for the countryman he is rather than the seaman he aspires to be; the inevitable consequence being that he upended more than once on his way to the boat. This indignity was made so much worse when, on his third and final attempt to achieve a backwards somersault on the jetty, his hand went through the gap between two of the planks and he discovered the hard way, on withdrawing it, that barnacles tend to favour these inside edges, where they can remain undisturbed for many months between my periodic clear-outs with the edge of a spade.

John ended up with a good deal of blood on his wrist – and no wristwatch. The watch had sunk to the bottom of the fourth upright from the end of the jetty, which is a three-foot wide section of cement drainage pipe set on its end and half-filled with silt and stones. Not the best place to lose a watch, especially when the only access is effectively blocked by the jetty itself. We peered between the planks: nothing.

We spent, I thought, a commendable amount of time fishing with bent coat hangers taped onto broom shafts, and tiny improvised grappling hooks on string, without success; and then John asked me if I owned a magnet. Sorry, I said; but I know a man who does. Some years ago my bother David had given something called a Sea Searcher to my uncle Dennis as a Christmas present. This handy tool – basically a very powerful magnet on the end of a rope – is designed for

retrieving lost anchors and the like. Very promising. We all piled into the dinghy and went in search of my uncle. As it happened, he too was out in his dinghy, crossing the sound between Dunsey Island and the mainland – that's to say, as we travelled from south to north, he was travelling east to west on a course that would take him across our bow, from right to left. The rule is to give way to a boat on your starboard bow, and as always when my uncle is about, I was keen to observe the proper rule. I swung pre-emptively, obviously, to starboard. Others in his situation, particularly on busy weekends in summer, have swung doubtfully to port at the very moment I have gone to starboard, which is like one of those situations where you meet someone on the pavement and both of you go the same way, except with more serious consequences. It tickled me to see that on this occasion the two of us were in perfect agreement: he maintained his course and I passed around his stern and came alongside, without mishap.

He told us where to find the magnet ashore, and when we got back to the cabin we spent another fifteen fruitless minutes, on the edge of dark, fishing from the jetty. We tried dropping the magnet from a height, swinging it in a slow circle, dragging it in straight lines

to and fro; all to no avail. I was about to leave John to it, when he reminded me that Dennis had said something about a cover; and on closer inspection we discovered that there was a little steel plate covering the business end of the Sea Searcher, which slid off after some determined levering with a screwdriver. Suddenly, anything steel within a foot and a half of the magnet found it irresistible, and we knew we were dealing with a prodigiously powerful tool. We redoubled our efforts, but the water inside the pipe was now so thick with disturbed silt that we were effectively working blind, and if the watch had been sitting near the surface a few minutes ago, it had no doubt been battered deep beneath it by subsequent dredging operations. The tide was coming in, the water level in the pipe was rising and I had in any case had enough, so I headed up to the cabin; but John persisted for a while longer, and although the photograph on page 145 was taken in daylight, my abiding memory is of his silhouette against the night sky, bowed but unconquered, and the plop, plop, plop of the magnet below his feet.

That we never did find the watch means only that its recovery has been postponed. In the next few months I intend to strip back the last few sections of jetty and rebuild them, as some of the timber uprights are rotten beyond repair; and when I do, I shall sift the contents of the pipe. I expect the watch will still be telling the correct time. If it wasn't a good watch, John would hardly have taken so much trouble to look for it.

If it turns out to be digital, with a black rubber strap, £2.99 with ten litres or more of unleaded, the other John Hawkins and I will have to have a talk.

Readings

No matter how often I do them, I find public readings a bit of a trial. As each event approaches I become even more introspective than usual and retreat to a quiet corner of the cabin – that's to say, any corner – to spend an hour gathering my thoughts, sorting slides, scribbling one-line headings on a six-by-four index card. I'm sure Lynn can read the signs, and if she can't read them she can hear them, because I often read aloud to myself.

I used to imagine that readings were arranged by publishers for most of their authors; and when my first book was published imagined myself, unwilling but resigned, on a whistle-stop tour of the book chains of Ireland, and perhaps Great Britain, signing dozens of title pages, shaking dozens of hands and admiring dozens of copies of my book, lined up and faced out in expectation of a deluge of eager buyers.

But in fact publishing a book, to the bitter dismay of almost every first-time author I have spoken to, is mostly about just that – publishing a book. Getting it stocked, noticed, featured, reviewed – above all, sold – is a whole other area, and very much a joint exercise between author and publishing house. This is not unreasonable, as smaller publishers can't afford to bet big on the roulette wheel of the public's notoriously fickle reading habits – it just hadn't occurred to me.

A publisher, months before a book is launched, will prepare advance information – bibliographic details, blurb, draft cover, marketing plan and, if it's positive, the publisher's assessment of what is often called the 'promotability' (ie. the media-friendliness) of the author – for their sales reps, and this material is used to secure orders from bookshops and other retailers. Those on the receiving end of this sales and PR effort – the central buying departments of the big chains, the bookshop managers and so on – will make individual judgements as to whether it's worth stocking your book, writing about it or, best of all, lifting the phone and talking to you about it personally. And none of these things can be taken for granted. It's entirely possible that there will be no media coverage and that those few copies of a given book which are ordered by the bookstores will languish, spine-out, in ones and twos in overcrowded shelves for a month or two, before being sent back, in line with the industry standard arrangement of sale or return, to the publisher's warehouse. Disappointing for the publisher, devastating for the author.

My father as PM. I still have the pen!

I was lucky in that a good many newspaper and magazine editors found an angle in *The Blue Cabin* in which they felt their readers, or audience, might be interested, running stories which pointed up the inauspicious start, the life less ordinary or the restorative qualities of our island existence, and giving bookstores the confidence to make significant orders. But nothing, as Willie Nelson says, lasts forever (except an old Ford and a natural stone); and I felt that the only way to maintain the currency of the book was to go out and tell people about it. So I put together a slide presentation, chose three or four extracts that were sufficiently self-contained to bear reading in isolation, and went knocking on bookshop doors, suggesting readings, talks, slide shows – anything that might encourage word-of-mouth sales and extra stock orders. The response was almost universally positive – every link in the publishing chain appreciates a proactive (though not a pushy) author – and one thing led to another so that I ended up reading not only in bookstores but at business groups, libraries, private reading groups and even the Women's Institute.

I have to say that when it comes to public speaking, I am positively *not* a chip off the old block. Robert Ramsay, in his thoughtful, entertaining and refreshingly myth-busting autobiographical account of the early seventies, *Ringside Seats: An Insider's View of the Crisis in Northern Ireland*, summed up my father's ability in this area as follows:

> He cut an impressive figure at the despatch box: immaculately suited, polished shoes gleaming, prematurely silver hair trimmed to the millimetre; and his body language speaking loudly of relaxed self-confidence. His clear and decisive delivery was equally impressive, and his ability to think on his feet and take part in the cut and thrust of the parliamentary rough-house was outstanding. My admiration for his skills at the despatch box and in the television studios was to grow rapidly when I came to realise how rapidly he assimilated his brief and how little time he took to prepare himself for even the most gruelling of public performances.

Ramsay was my father's Principal Private Secretary, on and off, for several years and probably knew him better, politically speaking, than anyone. Within the family, their mutual respect and indeed affection were taken for granted, not least because they shared something which, in my father's case at least, may have been subjugated in his public persona to a perennially pressing need to get the job done: that's to say, a ready sense of humour.

Which bears on one aspect of meeting potential readers face to face at readings that has given me a great deal of pleasure. Someone, often several people, will come forward afterwards to say how much they thought of my father and how badly he has been missed in Northern Ireland. Generally, they mean the cross-party, cross-community cooperation at government level which is at the heart of the recent peace process, and how passionately he espoused its earliest, ill-fated incarnation thirty-five years ago. But it's often more personal than that. In my father's day there must have been more scope for direct contact between representative and constituent, because the stories that people tell me have as much to do with the man as the politician, and suggest, in different ways, the warmth, humility and fairness which were as much his stock in trade as were his more widely acknowledged talents in the areas of politics and statesmanship. How, for example, he fought to procure an adapted car for a disabled constituent; became instantly friendly with a famously feisty Ringhaddy man who introduced himself by letting down the tyres of the official car when he found it parked outside his window; and, on hot summer days, how he brought orange juice and biscuits from the cabin to share with the RUC men on island guard duty.

My father's ongoing presence has been a common thread at promotional events; beyond which, I never know what to expect. In 2003, Fourth Estate published an excellent compilation called *Mortification*, edited by Robin Robertson, of writers' tales of their public shame, mostly on the reading circuit. As an exercise in comparison, the book has been a great comfort to me. Someone, it turns out, has invariably had the same mortifying experience as me, only more so.

I did one event in a certain bookstore. It was in a shopping mall, and the reading was scheduled for 8 p.m. on a Tuesday. The mall closed at 6 p.m., so it's fair to say that if there wasn't an air of hushed expectancy when I arrived, there was certainly a hush. I left the car in one of 1,500 vacant spaces in a car park designed to accommodate 1,500 cars, nodded to a solitary security guard at the entrance to the dark and eerily silent mall, found the bookstore and rattled on the steel security curtain, which was three-quarters down. The manager –

a delightful chap whom I knew to be an enthusiastic ambassador for my book (gold dust for a first-time writer) – let me in, introduced me to his assistant and said with great confidence, 'Don't worry, I'm sure there'll be a good crowd: it's early days.'

While the assistant manager laid out wine bottles and glasses on the sales counter, I set up the slide projector and screen, organised a pile of books for signature later, gathered my thoughts – and kept an eye on the door. My mother had come along with me and was in her element, browsing new titles in the crime fiction section, and I remember thinking that as long as the manager's assistant didn't go home, I could count on an audience of at least three.

To cut a painfully long story mercifully short, I ended up reading to my mother, the manager and his assistant; Helen Wright, my ever supportive editor at Blackstaff Press, her husband and mother-in-law; and my two-strong legion of local fans, a couple who had read the book, seen the in-store posters and taken the trouble to come along, bless them, specially to hear me. On the way home my mother, for whom speech has become a challenge since she suffered a stroke four years ago, looked at me, smiled, and said with a shrug more eloquent than words: 'All grist to the mill.'

By contrast, seventy people turned up at Waterstones in Dublin, there was standing room only at Castle Espie Wildfowl and Wetlands Centre near Comber, and a hundred and twenty came to an Ards Area Women's Institute meeting in Ballywalter – though I have to say, I wasn't necessarily the main attraction: there was much business to be got through before I was introduced, and when I left the hall one of the members was doing stand-up from the stage I had recently vacated. Who said the WI was stuffy? Actually, since Tony Blair's encounter with this redoubtable organisation in 2000, I don't think many would be so patronising.

As I left the boat park on my way to that particular event, I got into conversation with one of the cruising club members, and it may tell a story that as we parted company it occurred to him to say, over his shoulder, 'Does anyone ever heckle you at these events?'

Dee Light Teardrop Caravans NI

As you can see from the photograph the teardrop caravan can be towed by even the smallest of cars.

As it is a lightweight 2 berth caravan – there is no need for a 4 wheel drive and the caravan can be moved easily by hand so no need to reverse into spaces – just wheel it in! This provides accommodation for 2 people and is ideal for travelling to sporting events/hobbies/holidays and can also be used for transporting light goods. Graphics can be a useful addition to advertise your business everywhere you travel.

I am a coachbuilder by trade and have previously built motorhomes but decided to build a teardrop having watched The Apprentice where the apprentices had to pitch these to the public, and also Ade in Britain where I first saw this type of caravan/trailer. I have operated my small business for many years from my home/workshop and my intent is to make these caravans to order to customers' specifications .

The model shown in the photograph incorporates a 12 volt Freeview TV/DVD – LED lighting throughout – a kitchen area at the rear and can be obtained in several different colours. Upholstered seating converts into a double bed measuring 6ft x 4ft approximately.

Overall dimensions – 10 ft in length 5 ft wide 5ft in height

Prices start from £2950. Model shown priced at £4750.

Harry Wilson

289 Killaughey Road
Donaghadee
BT21 0LY
harry_wilson289@hotmail.com

07919046472

The Long Row

Rowing a boat is like riding a bicycle, and having started very young and rowed a great deal as a teenager, despite the intervening years of lawyering, flat renovation and furniture retail from a base in the agricultural heart of landlocked Kinross-shire, I reckon I can get from A to B in most conditions. That's not to say I haven't run into trouble once or twice, and indeed when I'm off the island and return after dark, Lynn doesn't settle until she feels the shiver of the cabin floor as I put my weight on the first step to the veranda.

Her worries recently became more focussed. I was crossing the sound one evening against a wind gusting to gale force, but because it was from just east of south, the cabin, being under the northwest flank of Eagle Hill, was relatively protected. I knew that Lynn would be unaware that conditions just a hundred yards off the jetty were bad, and getting worse. Indeed, as I crossed the sound in stinging rain and an unexpectedly big sea, I saw her come to the living room window, peer out into the semi-darkness and disappear again towards the back of the room. Jessica was staying, and apparently the two of them were neck and neck in a game of Bananagrams.

I was grateful to get into the lee of Eagle Hill myself, and came alongside the jetty without much difficulty. I tied up, left the outboard running and dumped the gear at the top end, near the cabin, from where I could hear laughter and shouts of 'Peel! Peel!' as I made my way back down to the boat; but before I was halfway to the mooring, all sound from the cabin, even the thrum of the generator, was lost on the wind. The ebb current being at its height and the wind against it, there was a serious amount of wave out there. I approached from the north and grabbed the rowing boat which I had tied to the mooring, in flat calm conditions, early that morning. The two boats wallowed and corkscrewed beside one another

After tying up (not taken in ideal conditions)

while I made my way in drunken lurches to the bow, to tie off the With to the mooring chain – a less than amusing operation in which my weight caused the tip of the bow to come alarmingly close to the water in every trough – released the rowing boat's bow line, and reattached it to the centre thwart of the With.

So far so good, but I hadn't thought to go for my life jacket when I was at the jetty (don't tell my mother – I should have been wearing one all the way from the mainland); and by now conditions were so severe that for the first time in our entire island experience I fished out the phone from the pocket of my oilskins and dialled Lynn's number as a precautionary measure.

'Hi,' she said, as relaxed as you like. 'What's keeping you?'

'Can't you hear the wind? It's blowing a gale!'

'I can hear the wind,' she said, 'but it's not blowing a gale. It feels not too bad over here.'

'I'm at the mooring, and I'm about to row in. Can you keep an eye?'

By this time Lynn was standing at the rail of the veranda. I could see her silhouette against the front door, which was lying open. Her tone changed a little and she said, 'I can see you now. I see what you mean. What do you want me to do?'

She was speaking quietly from her position of relative shelter, whereas I was shouting at the top of my voice.

'I'll be there in a minute,' I yelled, 'but just in case, can you be ready to call the coastguard?'

I knew that I wouldn't be able to row directly to the jetty. That would be into the wind, and my chances would be better if I rowed across or before it, aiming to land somewhere on the foreshore north of the cabin. My worry, though, was that I might run out of steam or lose an oar before making the shore, and end up being blown through the anchorage and out the north entrance of Ringhaddy Sound into the lough proper – not an inviting prospect given that the sea would have had the entire southern half of the lough over which to build, and the ebb tide was at its fastest. And the boat was only eight feet long. And I wasn't wearing a life jacket.

Lynn tends not to lose her cool in a crisis.

'Okay,' she said.

Whether it was foolishness, I don't know – I think not – but I tied two fenders to my belt on short lengths of rope, chose my moment and sort of rolled over the gunwale and into the rowing boat. Still tied alongside the With, I set in the rowlocks and then the oar furthest away, and untied the bow line with one hand while holding the boats apart with the other. After taking a minute to psych myself up (sounds pathetic – am I an old sea dog or not?), I threw the rope behind me onto the duckboards and let go, causing the rowing boat to come round with the wind and drift sideways at some speed into the darkness.

I had the second oar seated in its rowlock in around half a millisecond, and began rowing furiously in the general direction of Islandmore, happy should I manage to hit it at any point along its half-mile length. When you try to row in a big sea, as often as not one or other of the blades doesn't break the surface of the water, and when it does it's with enough force to drive it far below. It's like leaning your full weight against a door which may or may not be open. If it is, and you find yourself rowing in mid-air, it will only be for half a stroke, because you're going to end up falling backwards into the bottom of the boat, dumped there by a conspiracy of gravity, momentum and sheer effort, and possibly lacking one or both oars entirely. In another situation, this frightening scenario might be amusing, or embarrassing, though hardly both together. One sunny afternoon not long enough ago, I catapulted myself backwards in front of twenty-five family and friends, many of whom were leaning on the rail with glasses of wine or cans of beer in their hands and not much else to look at; and all but one, with the kindest of intentions, compounded my discomfort by looking the other way when I walked up the jetty – and saying nothing. Only Mark, who is the husband of my brother's sister-in-law and no doubt considered it his twice-removed duty to throw me a jocular lifeline as I disappeared into the cabin to change my bottom half, made any comment at all. 'Probably not that good for the image,' he said as I sidled past him, keeping my sodden backside to the wall.

Well it's another situation altogether when a gale is lifting the boat out of the water, it's getting on for pitch dark and the only people in view are not just interested, but seriously interested in following your every movement. Not a good time to lose concentration, or the oars, and I'm happy to say I did hold on to both. I consider it a triumph to have made the shore at all that night, albeit two or three hundred yards from the jetty. I've never been more relieved to run aground, and couldn't have cared less whether it was on shingle, stones or even hard rock. The rowing boat touched bottom just once and then scudded northwards, grounding, finding deeper water, grounding again; so I abandoned ship, took the bow line over my shoulder and waded knee-deep through the shallows in the direction of the cabin.

By dry land, I was five minutes from home. In the water and in darkness, with the boat following most reluctantly behind, catching every boulder and shoal, twice pulling me onto my knees, it took considerably longer. I was whipped by the time I got to the jetty, where Lynn was pacing up and down, phone in hand. She took the rope from my outstretched hand.

'Next time,' she said brightly, 'why not forget about coming ashore and go back to the mainland in the With? Better to arrive late than not at all.'

There's no answer to that really.

Tom Hawkins

First island summer, 1970

My Side of the Island

After Pittenweem, Lynn normally allows herself some down time, with the result that the end of August/beginning of September has become the visitor season by default. Of course, friends and family come and go throughout the year – Easter, Halloween and New Year are all conveniently themed pretexts – but that late summer season of long days and warm evenings, when the photograph album swells and Ringhaddy Sound is the sound of children's voices, will probably, like *Swallows and Amazons*, charm us years from now into wondering whether island summers lasted for ever.

Lacking one ourselves, we are fortunate that so many of our friends have young families, on whom it quickly dawns that having crossed by boat to an island – a real one, otherwise you wouldn't be able to walk to the top of Eagle Hill and see water on every side – they have stepped into an adventure story which they get to write themselves. I remember the same feeling, aged twelve, on my first visit to Islandmore in 1969. My father had arranged for Bob Scott (Ringhaddy's resident boatman, shipwright and factotum before his son John took over) to ferry the family across in his converted lifeboat *Horsa*, with our rowing boat tied astern. The lower half of the jetty was just two planks wide then, with battens nailed crosswise at intervals, an arrangement which in terms of grip was useless for shoes but ideal for seaweed, which hung from the walkway in luxuriant drapes. The grass between the sea wall and the cabin was weedy and long, enclosed by a sagging sheep-wire fence which was approximate at best, and only approximately served to confine the sheep to the rest of the island's one hundred and twenty acres, over which they roamed at will. The contrast between the wilderness immediately around the cabin, and the kind of crew cut everywhere else which only sheep or goats can achieve, is one of my earliest impressions of Islandmore. That, and the smell of the cabin itself, which like new-mown hay, or a horse barn in the high desert, defies description. It's the smell of *cabin*.

That my imagination was so readily fired, I owe to a book I had recently devoured at school. I was a reluctant and unhappy boarder, and to soften the blow of each new term my mother used to secrete little surprises in my suitcase – a bag of sweets, a little notebook in a plastic cover, with fold-out compartments and its own tiny brass pen. Occasionally, there was something specifically from my father, and the most enduring was a book by Jean Craighead George called *My Side of the Mountain*, about a boy who runs away from home and learns to live by his wits in the Catskill Mountains of New York State. He befriends an eagle, whittles fish-hooks from bits of wood and sleeps in the hollow trunk of a massive oak tree; and when I first landed at the cabin I felt I had landed the opportunity to *be* Sam Turkin for the duration.

My Side of the Mountain cemented a growing love of the great outdoors. When it occurred to me to mention the book here, I googled the author and was surprised, given that she was first published in the 1940s, to discover how prolific she has been since, and that she is still writing. I sent her a thank you message, belated by forty years, in which I mentioned that because her book had so inspired me as a youngster, I intended to send for the whole trilogy (of which it was the first part) and give it to my godson Harry Hawkins in the hope that although he is a little young to appreciate it just now, he might stumble upon it when he is (heavens) twice his current age of five, and get as much out of it as I did. Her reply, from upstate New York, magicked by the Internet in a couple of hours, began, 'What a life you lead!' and ended on my auspicious last name. Evidently Faulkner is one of her favourites – I want to say 'favorites' – and I was able to reply that I had recently re-read *As I Lay Dying*. I had enjoyed it so much more at fifty than at fifteen, and had finally been able to come to terms with the fact that although I have often quoted its shortest and most memorable chapter – 'My mother is a fish' – I still don't have a very clear idea what the chapter means:

some online research revealed that no one else does either.

The only downside of my plans for the mountain trilogy was that this book is due to be published in October, and Harry's birthday is in November. Normally quite careful when it comes to secrets, I could see that putting an announcement in print and having it distributed to bookshops wasn't the best way of keeping one; so we knew we would have to get him something else to avoid disappointment. A doohickey, perhaps, or a waddyacallit.

The previous November, we had sent Harry a telescopic fishing rod to mark the occasion of his first catch a few weeks before (a good-sized mackerel which put a smile on his face at the end of a rather cool and pitchy trawl outside the south entrance to Ringhaddy Sound, during which his older brothers had already caught one apiece). In due course, to supplement the moral and religious instruction which of course John and Emma expect of me as Harry's godfather, I intend to take him fishing, just the two of us; and I'm hopeful that if I can show him a good enough time in the one area, I might win dispensation in the other.

Certainly, Harry has always been easily enough pleased. When we all decided to build a pirate ship, and went in search of materials, he was happy to step back and take a

Harry's role was mainly supervisory. Here, he heads
towards his brother having successfully supervised his
mother.

174

supervisory role, something between team leader and Sir Alan Sugar. Sam had spotted an orange drum under a hedge in Pawle Sound, which we retrieved by boat. It had a big black 'X' on the side, probably the international symbol for sulphuric acid or toxic waste. Under Harry's watchful eye we assembled several more drums, two pallets and a colourful collection of ropes; and in no time we had the bones of a working prototype laid out on the foreshore.

The final design was more Robinson Crusoe than Jack Sparrow, but it did have a skull and crossbones and a drum given up by the sea which, on account of its hideous and terrifying contents, *must remain sealed for all time*. Actually, the orange drum was so much bigger than the others, there was no obvious place for it in terms of floatation. Emma was keen that it should be used anyway, and even when Harry and I explained that as a girl, his mum couldn't be expected to understand the essentially guys' business of marine engineering, she persisted – so on went the orange drum; and I have to say that had the rest of the drums taken in water, or the ship foundered, it might have come into its own as the only thing remaining on the surface to which survivors could reasonably expect to cling.

When it was finished we had an impromptu launch-out ceremony on the shingle in front of the cabin, and Sam and Tom clambered aboard. Harry, his expression prophet-like and serene, positioned himself between Lynn and his parents to watch, and I fetched the With and motored carefully into the shallows, throwing the boys a long line and telling them to make fast. I may have added, 'Me hearties'.

I towed them – pirate ship, captain and crew – slowly out into the middle of Ringhaddy Sound, and when we reached the point where the tidal run was at its strongest, I untied my end of the rope, dropped it in the water and set sail for home, ignoring the castaways' piteous pleas for mercy as they drifted south with the ebb. I looked up at the others, who by now were standing in line at the edge of the veranda. John and Emma were laughing, Lynn had that slightly questioning smile which says, 'They *are* okay, aren't they?'; and Harry, for whom everything had unfolded as it should, was nodding sagely.

Rory

Grey heron

Jack and Others

Gin Hardy and my mother have been friends since their time together at the BBC (Mum was Northern Ireland Governor from 1979–85); and knowing Mum's perennial passion for books, Gin has turned up at her door at Seaforde with all kinds of interesting reading material. Most recently, it was a history of Elm Park Preparatory School, written by Sean Barden and published by the Ulster Historical Foundation. My father attended Elm Park from 1930–35 and we spent a couple of hours scanning the young faces in the photographs for those who would later become family friends, political colleagues and so on. There were quite a few and many, I'm glad to say, are still with us. My father is there, one of twenty-nine pupils in 1935, smiling more broadly at the camera than anyone else and even then, as they used to say, 'well presented'.

One thing struck a chord with me. Two of the pupils – Christopher Cowdy and Roly Cunningham – are pictured holding pet birds, and it took me back to my own time at Mourne Grange Preparatory School For Boys in the late 1960s. At Mourne Grange my keenest interest was in the school ponies, who grazed the undulations of the football field and were led in on Wednesday afternoons to be brushed off and saddled up in front of the tack room, which was the ground floor of a two-storey stone outhouse behind the cloisters. Above the tack room, accessed from outside by a steel ladder set into the cobbles, there was a loft space that had apparently once been the living quarters of the school groundsman; and a picture comes to mind of a slightly built, rather quiet eleven-year-old with sticking-out ears, perched in the doorway of the loft with his feet on the top rung of the ladder and a young jackdaw, rescued, restored and having the kind of quirky and imaginative name which would have echoes forty years later in our choice of 'George' for the seal and 'Mr Heron' for the heron (his name was Jack), perched on the rung below.

Common terns

Clockwise from top left: Common terns; cormorant; Brent geese, Ringhaddy Sound; Grey heron

When Jack flew off one day and didn't return for the crushed oats I used to leave on a broken plate inside the window, I felt the urge to go and look for him; and that urge has never really left me. I have been fascinated by birds ever since, and when the publishers agreed to this project, I was in my element: the photographs on the following pages in particular, however imperfect, are the fruits of a labour of love.

It's an uncomfortable truth that a boat offers the same opportunities for getting close to seabirds as the horse offered plains Indians the opportunity to stalk buffalo. Before the horse, buffalo were run over the cliffs in their hundreds,

Cormorant, homeward bound

Mr Heron, leaving the jetty

a labour-intensive, brutal and thoroughly inefficient means of filling the fridge; and without the boat, I would have had to rely on time, infinite patience and a very long lens. But with a favourable wind, depending on the species and the time of year, it's possible to have the kind of close encounter from a boat which would be unthinkable on dry land.

For three summers now, a pair of Common terns has returned to our raft, which is tied to a mooring buoy just north of the jetty. This year, in the first week of April, the raft disappeared during the night and after a couple of fruitless circuits of Islandmore and its immediate neighbours, I had to admit that it was probably gone for good. Bad timing, because the terns normally arrive towards the end of the month. Encouraged – I use the word loosely – by Lynn, who couldn't bear to see them homeless, I built a replacement, and no sooner was it

Canada geese

in the water than the terns showed up, a full fortnight early.

It's always good to see them because terns, like an open fire, can be hypnotic to watch. For several weeks, the male fishes the Islandmore shoreline to and fro with dogged commitment, diving once or twice on every run; and by and large the female sits on the raft, waiting to be fed. In due course they mate, and then there is a long interval through early summer when they share the incubation of a clutch of two or three brown-mottled, pale blue eggs on a neighbouring island. We see less of them, and only one bird at a time. I discovered where they nest by watching their dusk departures through binoculars from the summit of Eagle Hill. A tern's nest hardly deserves the name, being little more than an indentation in the shingle above high water, often in a gap between drifts of seaweed or clumps of coarse grass. Only when the young have left the nest and flown for the

Oystercatchers, Dunnyneil

first time, around the end of June, do both adults return to our raft – after which we have the pleasure of their company until the end of September.

To get close enough for a reasonable photograph, I waited until both birds were on the raft and the sun was low in the sky. They have come to tolerate us quite well, even when we motor past and set their platform rocking; and intrigued to know just how close they would allow me to come, I decided to forego the outboard and sit quietly on the stern locker of the boat, with the camera and tripod in front of me on the floor, allowing the boat to drift past them on the breeze – hopefully within fifteen or twenty feet. I stepped in and set up, and as I moved around the boat the male bird gave me a gentle warning – *tik tik tik* – and shuffled around the raft, placing himself between me and his mate and stretching his neck to fix me with a serious sideways stare. I untied the bow rope and pushed off from the jetty; then concentrated on the camera, getting off a few nice shots as I drifted closer. Now that a hierarchy had been established, both birds seemed able to relax; they went back to preening themselves, taking less and less interest in me and filling more and more of the viewfinder.

In due course, I felt a slight thud, and raised my head to find that the boat had come to rest against the raft. The terns seemed close enough to touch, and we took the measure of one other in full colour and high definition – I was even able to make out the deep brown of their eyes, which appear as black from a distance. The telephoto lens refused to focus, which tells a story as the minimum focussing distance is four feet, and even when I fished in the camera bag for another, it seemed to me that the male bird kept only a casual eye, and the female wasn't even interested, at one point turning her back until I was outside her field of view entirely. Eventually, the bow came round on the breeze and the boat parted company with the raft. I said a quiet thank you, waited until I was well away before starting the outboard and took a long, left-handed sweep towards the middle of the sound. I didn't want to push my luck by trying the same trick again, and after taking one or two photographs with the cabin in the background, left them in peace.

To be honest, I found the whole encounter quite affecting: like anyone who has watched them in action, I'm a little in awe of terns anyway and I felt as though I had been admitted, if only for a few minutes, to some kind of exclusive fraternity.

It isn't always so easy. I have spent hours at anchor in the half-light, waiting to catch the lapwings on a shingle spit at the north end of Pawle Sound; crawled through the long grass to try to get the better of the Canada geese (after twice being rumbled by a sentry bird I succeeded on the third attempt); and toured the islands for half a day looking for Sandwich terns, which don't come to Ringhaddy, eventually finding two pairs on rocks off Salt Island at the Quoile.

It goes without saying that the rewards are worth the effort, and whether the birds oblige or not, there is nothing like a low-speed, open-ended putter in the dinghy of a warm, still evening on Strangford Lough, with darkness gathering and the odd cormorant or eider flying in fast and low to roost.

Lapwings, Sliddery Bay

Gull's Eye View

Our friends Simon and Namaste Bevan's arrival by helicopter was a moment of high excitement for Lynn and me, and sweet success for Simon, who had managed, by skilful misdirection and a great deal of secret planning, to spring the surprise of a lifetime on Namaste just an hour and a half earlier in Argyll, a hundred and twenty miles away to the northeast. The helicopter trip – to wherever – was a wedding gift from Simon's cousin Tim which was simply redeemed a little late, on the occasion of their tenth anniversary.

We had been in touch the previous day with the dispatcher in Aberdeen, who had asked us to provide coordinates and some visual markers for a suitable landing site. After some discussion with William McFerran, whose permission was required (and freely given) to land on the island at all, we agreed that a small field to the northeast of the derelict farmhouse a quarter of a mile away would be ideal, there being no sheep, trees or any other obvious obstructions there. On the morning of the trip I gave the site a final inspection and tramped out a circular helipad in the long grass, to the great delight of Eddie, who had never been walked in such tight concentric circles and would happily have gone on all day.

Lynn and I were doubly excited because Simon had arranged for us to go up ourselves, which for me at least, would be the fulfilment of a long-held ambition; and as there was room for six including the pilot, we added celebration to celebration by offering the extra place to my nephew Rory as a twenty-first birthday present.

The ETA, according to the dispatcher, was 8 p.m., and on the assumption that our guests would have bags to carry, we decided to use the boat to get as close as possible to the landing site. Rory was to come to the pontoons for around 6.30

that evening, which would give us time to relax at the cabin before heading round. At 6.20 Simon sent us into a blind panic by texting that they were in the air, and would be with us by 7 o'clock. We dropped everything, ran down the jetty and jumped into the boat, calling Rory at the same time.

Fortunately, Rory is to timekeeping what NASA is to space travel, and was already driving into the boat park. We executed a nifty running pick-up from the pontoons, crossed the sound and found a piece of foreshore that was steep enough to ensure that the boat wouldn't be high and dry when we returned – then walked over to the little field which Eddie and I had so painstakingly prepped a few hours before. We perched on a five-bar gate overlooking the helipad, and waited, our hearts thumping and our eyes fixed on the eastern horizon.

The distinctive beat of the rotor blades came first; then the helicopter appeared to the northeast, banked right and swung in low towards Islandmore – searching, so we thought, for the landing site. We waved with huge enthusiasm, and it seemed to us that the pilot must have spotted us, because after flying past he turned right at the southern tip of the island and came by in the opposite direction, following the line of Ringhaddy Sound to our west. Then he swung back over the island once more, and we stood up and waved with both arms. Our cheers were drowned by the sound of the engine as he lined up the helicopter, flew slowly, deliberately towards us – and kept going, dipping behind the summit of Eagle Hill and looking for all the world as though he was going to land somewhere else entirely. Which indeed he was: in a few moments the revs subsided, the motor died and we found ourselves looking at each other and listening to the silence, which by virtue of the contrast, seemed absolute.

I called Simon's mobile. 'Where are you?' I said. 'Everything okay?'

'Just what I was going to ask you. We're on the foreshore in front of the cabin. Martin thought it was as good a place as any.'

Best-laid plans. 'Don't be going anywhere,' I said. 'We'll be right there!'

We retrieved the boat and motored back along the island's western shore; and as the cabin came into view I actually felt a sense of relief that

No wonder Martin chose the foreshore as a landing site . . .

Lynn and our nephew Rory wait at the landing site that wasn't

communication between dispatcher, pilot and welcome party had been so comprehensively scrambled, because a helicopter on the foreshore is not something we're likely to see again for a while; at least not until Lynn wins the Turner and I receive a call from Richard and Judy.

Greetings, explanations and a highly animated reprise from Namaste, for whom time and distance would never be the same again, were conducted on the jetty; and then we were introduced to Martin, the pilot. It isn't something she had dwelt on up to that point, but to be honest Lynn had had slight reservations all along about taking up the offer of a flight, mistrusting helicopters and her stomach in equal measure. But there was Martin, walking towards us with his

Martin, the pilot, and behind him from left to right, Simon, Namaste, Lynn and Rory

arm outstretched, a genial smile on his face, the picture of relaxed self-confidence; and when you added the flier's shades, the navy trousers, the open-neck shirt with button-down breast pockets, and the all-important epaulettes, a spin around the lough at a thousand feet suddenly seemed like something you would do before breakfast, to set you up for the day.

Martin told us they were helpfully keeping the airfield at Newtownards open to allow him to refuel for the return flight, so there wasn't much time to waste. We climbed aboard and took off into a clear blue sky; and I can't remember having had so much fun, or taken so many photographs, in such a short space of time.

Strangford's River class; Glens top right

    As luck would have it, my brother David (Rory's dad) was at that moment racing the River yacht in which he has a part share, a couple of miles to the north, at Whiterock. Martin had given us each a pair of headphones and we were able so to direct him that he gave us a spectacular up-sun view of the entire class of Rivers, and the Glens behind them, in full sail. Rory pointed out *Glynn* among the eight boats below us, and we waved through the chopper's perspex door. Apparently David waved back, but racing is a serious business and we had no intention of adding a powerful downdraught to the rather feeble wind from which every boat would be trying to squeeze the last ounce of assistance, by flying close enough to see. We passed them by, and tried with only moderate success to count off the landmarks, so familiar from sea-level, which punctuated the return flight to Islandmore.

When we touched down again on the foreshore, Martin stayed with the aircraft and asked us to walk to the front, towards the cabin. Shouting above the din, I asked if he wouldn't mind waiting a few moments while I took photographs from along the foreshore, and he obliged by hovering above the cabin before climbing steeply away to the north, and Newtownards.

At one point, looking through the viewfinder, I was aware of something small and white shooting diagonally up from the cabin like a cork from a bottle, and when I joined the others on the veranda it turned out that the downdraught had set quite a few things in motion, including a canvas parasol which flew over the roof of the living room and landed in a crumpled heap beneath the trees. What I had seen out of the corner of my eye was the plastic sleeve which locates it in its base. Only later, when we reviewed the photographs, did we discover that I had inadvertently captured the moment: the parasol is in transit to the left of the cabin, nine-tenths inverted and at a jaunty angle, and the sleeve is heading over the roof in the opposite direction.

After such a buzz, it took half an hour and a glass of bubbly on the veranda to come back down to earth, and properly to welcome our guests. Then Rory had to head on, so I left him back to the pontoons. It being a beautiful summer's evening, there were quite a few boats about; and as there was little wind, several were tied up to the pontoons, their occupants doing, no doubt, more or less what we had just been doing on the veranda.

John and Angela Ley were there, entertaining in the cockpit of their yacht *Busy Bee*. Long retired, John used to be a journalist with the *Daily Express*. He always makes me think of my father, because their working relationship was such that for some time during the early seventies, John was able to scoop the other dailies by calling my father at home on a Sunday, bypassing the press office and coming away with a quote for Monday's edition. His colleagues, and more important his editor, were impressed by this direct line to the PM and wondered how he managed it; indeed I wondered myself, and when I asked him, self-effacing chap that he is, John told me that he really couldn't imagine. My own feeling, knowing both men, is that it's quite simple – my father was never ex-directory, John was able to combine boldness with charm, and they liked each other.

Anyway, John and Angela could hardly have missed the comings and goings of the helicopter on the other side of the sound, and as I pulled away from the pontoons John caught my eye, smiled and crooked his finger in my direction. Never one to miss a story. Half an hour and another glass or two later, I weaved my way back to the jetty, alcohol and adrenaline having joined me at the tiller.

We have relived the evening several times with Simon and Namaste, and we're not sure how to top their spectacular arrival the next time they pay us a visit; but Simon did mention a seaplane. Can't wait.

David aboard *Glynn*

Below: Claire, me, David and my mother,
Ringhaddy, 1971
Right: Lynn with her mother Marion

Above: My father at the cabin in 1971

Our niece and nephew, Tammy and Roy

Top: *Ptarmigan*
Middle: Lynn's sister Fiona on Long Sheelah
Bottom: Harry Hawkins
Right: Lynn, Jock and Rab

My uncle Dennis sailing *Coomara*,
Fairey Class, 1947

Top: Lynn
Bottom: My parents at the cabin *c.*1972
Left: Namaste and Eddie

207

Top: From Island Taggart
Middle: With Sarah Eccles on Long Sheelah
Right: Sam

208

Top: Angus Rock, at the mouth of the lough
Left: Lynn's sister Dalene

Autumn

Above and overleaf: The hall in Quilchena

The Quite Grim Reaper

A short while after coming to the island, we were given a book called *Zen Interiors*, by Vinny Lee, and were surprised to come across a full-page photograph of our hallway in Quilchena, the farmhouse in Scotland in which we spent our first ten years of married life.

Looking at the photograph, I can't but feel a twinge of regret because every inch is another passage in the story of our lives – and loves – over those ten years and before. Lynn and I spent a day scrambling on a forest floor near Penicuik to extract the fallen spruce, muddied and weathered, which forms the stair rails. The pitch pine treads started life in the round, as ballast on a North Atlantic sailing ship; were sawn and adzed to form the roof beams of an Edinburgh church; and finally became the defining feature of our stairway which, when the picture was taken, was three years old but hopefully looked a hundred. The coil pot was a wedding present from Dave and Sue Ashworth, my first and most consistent suppliers for the Edinburgh furniture business, and came from a roadside in Portugal. The braided nylon lariat, with which I learned to rope a steer, was a gift from a Canadian Indian named Jerry McCauley. The Mexican tiles were lovingly inserted by Lynn as a final flourish. The chair, with its sunburst carving, its downward-sloping arms and its hide upholstery, is of unknown provenance but always said to us, 'New Mexico'. And just visible at the top of the stairs, the row of leather-bound Victorian volumes, mostly on wildlife or North American exploration represents the tip of an iceberg of accumulated birthday presents spanning many years, from my mother, during her time as an antiquarian book dealer.

One last detail: if anyone ever says it's enough to use a wooden trowel, or a sponge, or the flat of your hand to produce a randomly textured plaster surface

Lynn and Jessica

– it isn't. You need all of these things and more, plus some sand, lime wash and paint; it helps to have good craftsmen on the job, like Dougie Cuthbert and Andy Bett; but above all you need Lynn, artist/perfectionist that she is, getting her hands dirty, standing back, trying yet another variation and saying, 'Hmmm – almost there, *but not quite . . .* '

Vinny Lee's book defines the guiding principles of Zen as balance, harmony and simplicity; and the chapter where the photograph appears is called, appropriately enough, Touch and Texture.

The hall at Quilchena, which doubled as a dining area, was the heart of the house and the venue, over the years, for all manner of entertaining; but one annual party, perhaps because it provided children with more scope than any

other, was always the best. Tricked out for the last Saturday of October, with bats and bobbing barrels; bloodshot eyeballs made from lychees, halved grapes and red dye; and a speciality of Lynn's which for obvious reasons has featured in Islandmore Halloweens since – a lucky dip barrel filled with seaweed from the Firth of Forth through which little hands searched in frenzied competition for prizes like slimy rubber snakes and magic potions – the hall took on many qualities, but Zen wasn't one of them.

At one witching hour, as our guests prepared to leave, I slipped out the back door and into Lynn's cavernous studio; wrapped myself in a black curtain which we normally used as a backdrop for photographing her paintings, and which was big enough to form into a hood at one end and trail the ground at the other; donned a black mask; grabbed my scythe (a real one – in those days, fresh from central Edinburgh, when life was a pioneering odyssey, I eschewed strimmers and the like in favour of men's tools); walked under cover of darkness to the end of our lane and two or three hundred yards along the road; stood on the top of a bank under a leafless oak – motionless, be-scythed, be-cloaked, so scary I was a little scared myself – and waited. I didn't even turn my head as one by one the cars came by, slowed down momentarily and then – literally – screamed off, full of deeply traumatised children, into the night. Only one car stopped. The driver's window came down and I swivelled my eyes to the right, determined not to move another muscle. Ewan Chalmers's grinning – grimacing? terrified? – face was partly illuminated by the dashboard's ghostly glow. 'Night Mike,' he said, and drove off.

I tried the same trick during an island Halloween some years ago, walking to the end of the jetty wearing the same cloak. After an agreed interval, Lynn screamed and pointed through the living room window; but sadly, partly due to the relative isolation of the cabin and partly because kids tend to grow older, island Halloweens aren't as well attended as Quilchena ones were, and one of the three children present distinctly remembered an identical Grim Reaper standing beside the road between Cleish and Crook of Devon several years before. 'Look everyone, Mike's standing at the end of the jetty' wasn't the reaction I had hoped for, and my confidence as an undead shape-shifter, already dented by Ewan Chalmers, was shattered forever.

On the plus side, Lynn carves a mean pumpkin: ask anybody, especially one of the many wannabes, from age three to three score and ten, who have competed with her, or learned from her, at the kitchen table over the years. Having driven the blazing back roads of Massachusetts in the Fall and seen for myself, in porches and village squares, the amazing variety of pumpkin heads, corn dollies and general witchery that Halloween inspires, I can say that no one, not even the New Englanders, who have defined and refined the season over many generations, and who cheat anyway by throwing in Thanksgiving, can compete.

If I seem to have lost the knack of frightening the wits out of small children, at least I can enjoy the expressions of wonder and awe when one of Lynn's scarier pumpkin heads is placed on the rail of the veranda, candle-lit from within and backed by the Stygian night, and the deep, silent waters of Ringhaddy Sound.

Pawle Island from Eagle Point, Islandmore

Canada geese

Polar Bear Pass

In Canada's Northern Arctic Archipelago, where most of the islands are snow-covered for most of the year, there is a small area (actually somewhat larger than County Down) on one island which is described by geologists as an Arctic oasis surrounded by polar desert – and as such, in strictly relative terms, represents an attractive natural habitat. Having said that, being just two hundred kilometres south of the geographic North Pole, it is an extremely hostile environment to which few species have learned to adapt.

The island is Bathurst, and the area, Polar Bear Pass, comprising rock-strewn tundra and wetland, and supporting just enough vegetation for transitory visitors during the short summer, and a few die-hard year-round residents like musk ox and caribou, and of course their predators: polar bears, arctic wolves, eagles. Bathurst has the largest concentration in the High Arctic of the endangered Peary Caribou, now reduced to less than a thousand individuals. This diminutive reindeer is named after the American Arctic explorer Rear Admiral Robert E. Peary, whose claim to fame, now in doubt but credited for most of the last century, was the first sighting of the geographic North Pole.

I mention Polar Bear Pass in particular, because it is the summer breeding ground of a good proportion of the world's population of Brant geese, known to us as Brent and specifically, Pale-bellied Brent. Towards the end of August, prompted by lowering temperatures and the shortening day, scattered groups of Brent geese come together in the more sheltered areas of Bathurst to graze alongside the Caribou, coalescing into immense migratory flocks which set off on a three-thousand-kilometre journey across the Greenland ice-cap and the fjords of western Iceland, to their winter home of Strangford Lough. In flight, they form enormous V-shaped constellations several hundred birds strong, in

Pale-bellied Brent geese

which every bird but one borrows the slipstream of the bird in front: the older, more experienced individuals playing tag at intervals to form the tip of the arrow, and work the hardest.

Strangford, between October and April, holds close to three-quarters of the world's population of Pale-bellied Brent geese. Most of them stay around the mudflats at the northern end of the lough, which provide the richest feeding, but small groups range elsewhere and I'm pleased to say that a dozen or so have spent much of their time in the last few winters in and around Ringhaddy, particularly during autumn and spring.

In whimsical moments, which is to say quite often, I look at these handsome, sturdy little second-homers, who leave us in early April but always return, and think, 'I know where you're coming from'. Strangford Lough is a hard place to leave. My grandfather sailed here, farmed some of the islands (including Islandmore) for a time, sold the lot – and years later bought a holiday home in Strangford village. My uncle, perhaps the most dedicated yachtsman in the family, holidayed on another island and eventually settled on the mainland northwest of Islandmore. And my father, twenty years after my grandfather called time on his farming adventure and allowed the cabin to pass out of family ownership, managed to buy it back and secure it, hopefully forever, as a place to which all of us can return, and keep returning.

On account of what George Wright, who has sailed for many years, refers to as 'the old inner ear', I am not a natural yachtsman, and neither is Lynn, so as far as sailing goes, it has been for others to carry the family flame. My brother David, obviously; but also my nephews Rory and Jamie, who are, respectively, sailing professionally and training to do so; David's eldest Lucinda, who as I write is considering the enthusiasts-only option of a wooden boat in which to enjoy the lough; and a little further removed, my cousin-in-law Niall, who fished the lough for a living before turning to horticulture, and eventually daffodils, in the 1990s.

In July of this year, to mark my birthday, we set out to achieve the most important return trip of all. Since her stroke, my mother has been largely

confined to a wheelchair, and although she has risen to the challenge of living at home, with (in order of importance) dogs, cats and family around her, she laughed when I first raised the idea of coming to Islandmore, thinking it a challenge too far. The cabin belongs to her, but it had been five years since her last visit and I suppose she had visions of coggly boats, makeshift ramps, slippery jetties – and electric wheelchairs which, to put it mildly, are not light. Even when I presented her with a self-inflating life jacket for her birthday, she thought the idea of crossing to the island far-fetched: romantic, even something to wish for in an abstract sort of way – but far-fetched. Still, she gave me to understand that if we were determined to give it a try, she would work with us to make it happen.

For me, it became a mildly obsessive project. I went ahead with preparations, building a raised deck for the boat and sourcing a special threshold ramp, flexible enough to form a workable bridge from the pontoons to the boat. Appropriately enough, since his grandfather had re-assembled the cabin ninety years ago after its short sea crossing from the Isle of Man, I called William McCloy, of McCloy's Builders' Merchants in Killyleagh, for exactly the profile of timber which would fill the gaps between the planks of the jetty at the Islandmore end, and prevent the bogey wheels of the wheelchair from slipping through. For the transfer from boat to jetty, I made a simple platform that rendered a fifteen-degree slope horizontal; and then it was just a matter of timing. The tide would have to be more than three-quarters in, at least for the trial run, and the departure from Islandmore would have to be before it was a quarter gone, giving us a window of opportunity of perhaps two and a half hours.

That everything came together for my birthday, I count as a special bonus. I said to Mum that morning, 'Let's give it a try,' and she replied with an old-fashioned look that said, at the very least, 'Are you sure?' Nevertheless, she was excited by the prospect, and we discussed the fact that nothing in life is without risk.

We drove to Ringhaddy with hope in our hearts, natural justice on our side, and the self-inflating life jacket on the back seat. Lynn was already on the island and had prepared, as only she can do, the most artful of picnics, complete with

birthday cake and candles: if we pulled this off, it was going to be an occasion to mark.

When we arrived at the boat park, I fetched the ramp and the platform from the boat shed and tied up to the sheltered side of the pontoon harbour. With everything in place, Mum and I made our way onto the concrete walkway that leads to the pontoons. We smiled and nodded to a number of fellow cruising club members on our way to the boat. All of them had seen the preparations and were fascinated to hear what I was about; and all of them, to varying degrees, were keeping a discreet – that's to say, a let's-not-make-a-fuss-but-the-club-lifebelt-seems-to-be-where-it-should-be – eye on events. I had no wish to make a drama of it, and as we approached the ramp I leant forward and asked Mum

if she was okay. She gave a thumbs up and pointed towards the boat, which rocked quietly against the pontoon, its temporary deck and flexible aluminium bridge sliding against one another with a gentle rasping sound – and I thought to myself, not for the first time, that if I have my mother's courage and spirit at eighty-four I will deserve to have made the journey.

We rolled on, or rather Mum rolled on. I kept my feet on the pontoon and when the wheelchair was more or less halfway across the boat, I knelt on one knee and reached forward to apply the brakes. Then I untied at the bow, stepped onto the dead centre of the stern locker, and pulled the ramp after me. For the second time, I asked if Mum was all right, but there was no need: perched high above the gunwales, she was, if anything, savouring the moment.

A coolish breeze was coming from the southeast, and I took off my oilskin jacket and put it across her shoulders. The sleeves billowed and lifted like wind socks, sending secret semaphore to the gods; and that's how we crossed Ringhaddy Sound, 'Like a stately ship of Tarsus bound for th'isles ... Sails filled and streamers waving' – like Delilah, and with equal triumph.

The roll-off went just as smoothly as the roll-on, and the three of us sat on the grass in front of the cabin with mugs of tea and birthday cake, under a hot sun, and celebrated. The dry run successfully completed, we resolved to get the whole family together as soon as possible, and complete the circle. I know that my mother had never thought to set foot on Islandmore again; but the island calls to all of us, and some things, like the heroic six-thousand-kilometre round trip of Strangford's geese, are as natural as the seasons, and as naturally recur.

Top: Geoff and Tammy
Middle: Lynn and sister Fiona
Bottom: Team Hawkins
Opposite: Lynn, Harry and Emma

Top: Digging for bait
Right: Haul-out at Ringhaddy

Above: *Family's Pride*
Left: Tom

235

Opposite: Emma and Harry
Top: Eagle Point

237

Top: The boat park at Ringhaddy
Bottom: Canada geese, Eagle Hill

Acknowledgements

Every book is a joint effort, but I now realise that an illustrated one involves even more than the usual amount of coordination and cooperation between author, publisher and designer, so I particularly want to thank Helen Wright, Patsy Horton and all at Blackstaff Press, as well as Keith Connolly of Tonic Design, for their skill and hard work in bringing the project together.

My thanks also to Isobel Dixon of Blake Friedmann Literary Agency; Patrick Taylor, who very kindly gave of his time at short notice to read the manuscript and comment on it (and couldn't resist the temptation to make a few suggestions at the same time, which turned out to be invaluable); the Arts Council of Northern Ireland; and once again my sister Claire and my brother David and his family – the cabin is there for all of us but Lynn and I are the ones who get to use it.

Last, and most important, my love and thanks to my mother and my wife Lynn, for their support and editorial guidance.